FODOR'S®

BEIJING (PEKING), GUANGZHOU (CANTON), AND SHANGHAI

1985

John Summerfield

FODOR'S TRAVEL GUIDES
New York

Copyright © 1985 by FODOR'S TRAVEL GUIDES
ISBN 0-679-01078-5 (Traveltex-edition)
ISBN 0-340-36238-3 (Hodder & Stoughton edition)

FODOR'S BEIJING (PEKING), GUANGZHOU (CANTON) AND SHANGHAI
has been abridged from
FODOR'S PEOPLE'S REPUBLIC OF CHINA 1985

All the following Guides are current (most of them also in
the Hodder and Stoughton British edition).

FODOR'S COUNTRY AND AREA TITLES:

AUSTRALIA, NEW ZEALAND AND SOUTH PACIFIC
AUSTRIA
BELGIUM AND LUXEMBOURG
BERMUDA
BRAZIL
CANADA
CANADA'S MARITIME PROVINCES
CARIBBEAN AND BAHAMAS
CENTRAL AMERICA
EASTERN EUROPE
EGYPT
EUROPE
FRANCE
GERMANY
GREAT BRITAIN
GREECE
HOLLAND
INDIA, NEPAL, AND SRI LANKA
IRELAND
ISRAEL
ITALY
JAPAN
JORDAN AND HOLY LAND
KOREA
MEXICO
NORTH AFRICA
PEOPLE'S REPUBLIC OF CHINA
PORTUGAL
SCANDINAVIA
SCOTLAND
SOUTH AMERICA
SOUTHEAST ASIA
SOVIET UNION
SPAIN
SWITZERLAND
TURKEY
YUGOSLAVIA

CITY GUIDES:

AMSTERDAM
BEIJING, GUANGZHOU, SHANGHAI
BOSTON
CHICAGO
DALLAS AND FORT WORTH
GREATER MIAMI
HONG KONG
HOUSTON
LISBON
LONDON
LOS ANGELES
MADRID
MEXICO CITY AND ACAPULCO
MUNICH
NEW ORLEANS
NEW YORK CITY
PARIS
ROME
SAN DIEGO
SAN FRANCISCO
STOCKHOLM, COPENHAGEN, OSLO, HELSINKI, AND REYKJAVIK
TOKYO
TORONTO
VIENNA
WASHINGTON, D.C.

FODOR'S BUDGET SERIES:

BUDGET BRITAIN
BUDGET CANADA
BUDGET CARIBBEAN
BUDGET EUROPE
BUDGET FRANCE
BUDGET GERMANY
BUDGET HAWAII
BUDGET ITALY
BUDGET JAPAN
BUDGET LONDON
BUDGET MEXICO
BUDGET SCANDINAVIA
BUDGET SPAIN
BUDGET TRAVEL IN AMERICA

USA GUIDES:

ALASKA
CALIFORNIA
CAPE COD
COLORADO
FAR WEST
FLORIDA
HAWAII
NEW ENGLAND
PACIFIC NORTH COAST
PENNSYLVANIA
SOUTH
TEXAS
USA (in one volume)

GOOD TIME TRAVEL GUIDES:

ACAPULCO
MONTREAL
OAHU
SAN FRANCISCO

CONTENTS

BEIJING

Beijing, or "Northern Capital"

Beijing is a curious place. It could be described as a village in search of a city and a city in search of a soul. Yet it has been in existence as a settlement for over 3,000 years, capital of the nation over many centuries, and center of power under the Mongols, the Ming, the Manchu, and now the Communists for a period spanning almost seven hundred years. Today it is the political, cultural, and administrative center of a resurgent China, home of eight million citizens, headquarters of the Communist Party, and seat of government.

Visitors to Beijing are often surprised at how little remains of the past empires. Other great capitals of the world, most of them in existence for a much shorter period than Beijing, often possess a grandeur and style that reflect their illustrious past. But in China relatively few historic buildings have survived the wars that have swept across the nation for centuries. Beijing, along with other important cities in China, has been sacked, looted, and burned innumerable times by countless armies. As a result, most of the old buildings that remain are from recent dynasties.

Beijing's heart is the old Forbidden City and its center, Tian An Men Square. Here the old power structure and the new sit side by side. It is here that millions of people gather for rallies and demonstrations, a sobering reminder of the vast population of this nation and its potential

1

strength. But there are happier celebrations here too: gay and colorful affairs with people dancing in the streets, banging drums, and clashing cymbals.

Beijing's artery is Chang An Boulevard, running east-west through the heart of the city. It is flanked on either side by modern buildings conveying no hint of Old China. Yet within a block or two you will come across fields of tiny gray houses, the skyline broken here and there by a factory or a block of apartments.

Beijing is a city of bicycles—there are millions of them. As the vast population cycles its way to and from work, the city is alive with the metallic ring of bicycle bells.

The streets off the main thoroughfare are thronged with people clad in blue or gray Mao suits, the women often wearing brightly colored scarfs or jackets. The crowds are orderly and good-natured, and harmony seems to prevail. You may walk in the streets with perfect safety, although you may draw curious stares from the Chinese citizens around you.

Beijing was once a walled city. There was a wall around the Forbidden City, one around the Imperial City which enclosed it, another around what was known as the Tartar City, and yet another around the southern portion known as the "Chinese" City. Most of the walls are gone now, having fallen into ruin over the years or demolished by the new regime to make way for roads. Most of the old gates are gone, too, but you will get an impression of their grandeur when you see the famous Tian An Men Gate and the beautifully restored Qian Men Gate, each standing at opposite ends of the Square of "Heavenly Peace." In your travels you will occasionally catch a glimpse of a part of the old wall or one of the few remaining towers still standing—all in a dilapidated state, but a reminder of the past splendor of Beijing.

You could spend days exploring the old Forbidden City; it was for over 500 years the center of imperial power in China. Then there is the magnificent Temple of Heaven, the most famous in all China and an architectural wonder. There is also the Bei Hai Lake with its dagoba-capped island, the forests in Coal Hill Park, and the sites of decaying temples and pagodas. There are beautiful parks to roam and pine-clad hills to climb.

The most exciting excursion of all is to the Great Wall, the only manmade structure said to be visible from outer space. Its construction was a remarkable achievement and a monument to the threat that China has faced for thousands of years: invasion from the north. Even today this fear persists. When you visit the Great Wall you will be seeing an object that has inspired the curiosity of people around the world for ages.

Then there are the majestic Ming Tombs, some restored but most splintering into ruin in a gentle area of hills and mountains not far from the Great Wall.

A visit to Beijing is not restricted to sightseeing. You will have the opportunity to indulge yourself in the capital of Chinese cuisine. Beijing's restaurants are world-renowned, and they will prepare sumptuous banquets that you will long remember. Then there are evening entertainments such as Chinese operas, Chinese and Western theater, music and dance concerts, the ballet, the circus, acrobatic troupes, sporting events, and the movies.

Doubtless, your memory of Beijing will be colored by the seasons. In winter the days are cold but sunny; in spring the city is transformed by green foliage; in summer the air is filled with hazy light and warmth; and in autumn the streets are paved with golden leaves. There is something here for you whatever time you visit.

History

The first recorded settlement in the area of Beijing was the city of Ji, which is known to have been in existence in the twelfth century B.C. The settlement was also the capital of the Kingdom of Yen (B.C. 723–221), before it was destroyed by Qin Shi Huang Di, the first emperor of unified China.

A town known as Yu Chou developed in the time of the Tang Dynasty (618–907) but was destroyed in 986 by the Liao. A city was then established on the site by the invaders; they called it Nan Jing, or "Southern Capital," to distinguish it from their northern capital in Manchuria. In the eleventh century it was renamed Yen Jing.

The Liao were in turn defeated by the Jin in 1135 and the name of the town was once again changed, this time to Chung Du.

The Mongols under the leadership of Kubilai Khan defeated the Jin in 1264 and built a new city on a site slightly to the north. They called it Da Du, or "Great Capital," also known as Khanbalic.

The Yuan Dynasty was swept out by the Ming in 1368 and the site became known as Bei Ping, or "Northern Peace," the capital being established farther south at Nanjing. The third emperor of the Ming, Yung Le, moved the capital back to the north in 1403 and rebuilt the city, naming it Beijing, or "Northern Capital." When the Manchu armies drove out the Ming the city was retained as the capital, and it remained so until the dynasty fell in 1911. The capital was then moved to Nanjing but was reestablished in Peking a few months later.

In 1928 the Nationalist Government established the capital in Nanjing once again, and Peking assumed its provincial role under the name of Bei Ping. However, it lost its status for only two decades, becoming the capital again after the Communists took the city on January 31, 1949. The Constitution of the People's Republic of China now declares that the capital of the nation is Beijing.

EXPLORING BEIJING

Tian An Men Square is the center of Beijing. It is a vast place, an enormous square by any standard in the world, occupying an area of almost 100 acres. The square derives its name from the imposing gate and tower on the north side, which give entry to the Imperial City and the Old Forbidden City within. The wide, tree-lined Chang An Jie, or Avenue of Perpetual Peace, runs east-west past the Gate, parallel to the old walls of the Imperial City. Against the walls permanent stands enable the nation's leaders to review parades and preside over the enormous rallies that take place in the square. When Chairman Mao died, over a million people gathered in the square to pay homage.

Tian An Men Gate

Tian An Men, or the Gate of Heavenly Peace, bounds the northern end of the square. It has five passages leading through it and is surmounted by a wooden tower with a double roof of glazed tile. Five marble bridges lead over the moat to each of the gateways.

Formerly the five passages were closed and used only on ceremonial occasions. Only the emperor could pass through the central passageway. Before leaving on a journey he would make a sacrifice before the gate. At other times imperial edicts were lowered, in a gilded box shaped like a phoenix, into the hands of officials kneeling below. The practice gave rise to the expression "the Imperial Orders given by the Gilded Phoenix." The edict was then taken to the Ministry of Rites, where copies were made for dispatch to the far corners of the empire.

Monument to the People's Heroes

Looking south to the Square from the gate you will see a tall granite obelisk standing on a two-tiered marble terrace with balustrades: it is the Monument to the People's Heroes. The gilded inscription on the north face is in Chairman Mao's calligraphy and reads: "The People's Heroes Are Immortal." The base of the obelisk is decorated with bas-relief carvings depicting major events of the revolution.

Great Hall of the People

The Great Hall of the People flanks the western side of the square; if you stand with your back to Tian An Men Gate it is on the right hand side of the square. The National People's Congress, China's parliament, sits here when it is in session. The Great Hall, an immense building covering an area of 561,800 square feet, was erected in just over ten months, although the interior took additional time to complete. It has numerous conference rooms, banquet halls, and reception areas, many of vast size: the major conference room accommodates 10,000 people and the huge banqueting hall can seat 5,000.

The Revolutionary Museum and the Historical Museum

Inside the buildings flanking the square to the east are situated the Museum of the Chinese Revolution in the left wing and the Museum of Chinese History in the right wing. If you have time, visit these museums. An excellent guidebook is available.

Chairman Mao Zedong Memorial Hall

Immediately behind the Monument to the People's Heroes is the Chairman Mao Zedong Memorial Hall. It occupies about 200,000 square feet of floor space, stands just over 100 feet high, the twin-roof being supported by 44 granite pillars. A wide stairway leads up to the entrance, over which appears the inscription, in Chairman Hua Guofeng's calligraphy, "Chairman Mao Memorial Hall."

As you enter the first auditorium you will be confronted by an enormous seated figure of Mao sculptured in white marble. Light falling on the statue creates an ethereal effect and the figure appears to be translucent and floating. The backdrop is an enormous landscape painted by Huang Yangyu, a well-known Chinese artist. The scene extends into the distance as if observed from a great height, perhaps to remind the visitor of Mao's revolutionary vision.

You then pass to the next auditorium where the body of Chairman Mao, draped with the red flag of the Communist Party of China, is preserved in a crystal coffin. The sarcophagus rests on a bier and is surrounded by flowers. brought from all parts of China. On either side of the room are pine trees, the old symbol of longevity, growing in ceramic pots.

From this room you enter a third chamber where you are confronted by a large marble screen. It is inscribed in Chairman Mao's calligraphy in the form of a poem, "Reply to Comrade Kuo Mojo." On leaving the last chamber you pass onto the rear terrace of the Memorial Hall and obtain a fine view of the Qian Men Gate.

The hall was completed in November 1977 and took ten months to construct. The Memorial Hall opens only occasionally, but a specific request for a visit by your group may be granted.

Qian Men Gate

At the southern extremity of the square stands the Qian Men Gate. This is one of the few remaining gates of the Imperial City Wall constructed under the Ming emperor Yong Le (1403–1425). In those days the top of the wall, wide enough to allow the passage of a man on horseboack, was protected by towers placed at regular intervals around the perimeter. All the original nine gates in the wall were protected in a similar way. A traveler arriving at the wall of the old city would pass through the first gate into an elliptical courtyard within the walls and would cross this to pass through the inner gate into the city itself. This double-gate system was of great value in repulsing enemy attacks: if the first gate was breached, the enemy would still find themselves outside the city wall and could be fired upon from the tower over the inner gate.

The original gates allowed goods and commodities to be brought into the city. One gate was used to transport grain, another wood, and yet another coal. One of the western gates was used by carters bringing spring water to the emperor's table from the Fragrant Hills outside Beijing; it was always transported at night to arrive cool. One gate, aptly named An Ding Men or Gate of Certain Peace, was used to carry away nightsoil, which was then treated near the Altar of the Earth outside the city before being used as fertilizer. One of the two northern gates, the Gate of Virtue and Victory, was used by the imperial army when embarking on a campaign. Experience had shown that almost all attacks had come from the north, a danger that the Chinese feel still exists today.

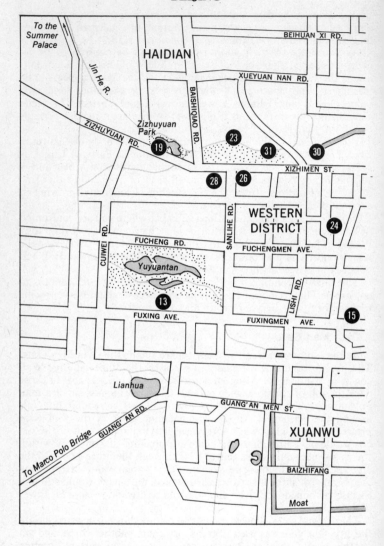

Points of Interest

1) Bei Tang
2) Bell Tower
3) Catholic Church (Nan Tang)
4) Department Store
5) Dong Tang
6) Drum Tower
7) Forbidden City
8) Great Hall of the People

9) Imperial College
10) Lama Temple
11) Liu Li Chang
12) Mausoleum of Mao Zedong
13) Military Museum of the Chinese People's Revolution
14) Museum of Natural History
15) Nationalities' Cultural Palace
16) National Art Gallery
17) Old Observatory

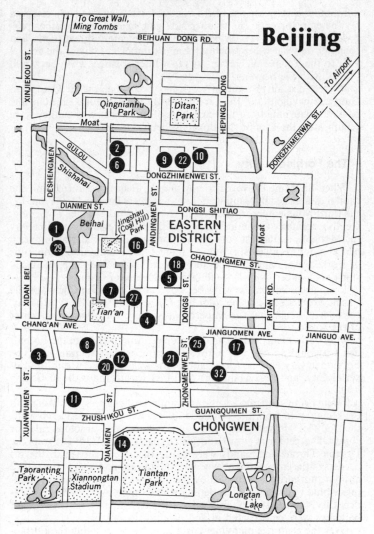

In imperial days the use of the central Qian Men Gate was reserved
for the emperor only, the smaller side gate being used for other purposes. The emperor would pass through the gate in great pomp and
splendor on what was probably the most important day of the year: a
visit to the Temple of Heaven at the winter solstice, when he would
"speak with the heavens."

A great deal of restoration work has been done on the Qian Men
Gate and pavilions and they are currently in beautiful condition. The
pavilions date only from the early part of this century when they were
rebuilt after the fires of the Boxer Rebellion in 1900.

The Forbidden City

When the Ming drove out the Mongols, Beijing was razed and the
capital established in Nanjing. Thirty-five years later in 1430 Yong Le,
the third Ming emperor, decided to re-establish the capital at Beijing.
He also decided to rebuild palaces on the site previously occupied by
the Mongols, and a vast construction program was undertaken over a
period of fourteen years, commencing in 1407. Hundreds of thousands
of workers were engaged on the project, and materials, particularly
stone and timber, were brought from all parts of China.

The palaces within the walls became known as Zi Jin Cheng, or the
Purple Forbidden City, the color being associated with the North Star,
considered a sign that the emperor's residence was the cosmic center
of the world.

Only occasionally would an emperor venture forth from the Forbidden City, and no one was allowed to enter without permission. The
Forbidden City with its formidable walls was enclosed within the Imperial City, and that again was enclosed within the walls of Beijing
itself.

Twenty-four emperors of the last imperial dynasties, the Ming and
the Qing, ruled from the Forbidden City. Each was considered to be
the "Son of Heaven" and controlled China with absolute rule for
almost five centuries, until the last dynasty fell in 1911. From the
Dragon Throne commands were made that were carried to the far
corners of the empire and obeyed without question. A sign of the ruler's
absolute authority is conveyed by the edict which states that no buildings would be constructed in Beijing which might overlook the Forbidden City's walls. It was only after the last emperor fell that larger
buildings were constructed in and around the city.

Over the centuries many new palaces were built within the Forbidden City walls and the others refurbished and renovated. Most of the
buildings now standing are from the eighteenth century. Inside the
secluded Inner Palace the emperors lived in splendor, amidst fabulous
treasure and wealth from the empire and abroad, surrounded by a court
comprising the empress, concubines, princes, eunuchs, court favorites,
priests, and ministers. Lavish living was a feature of their daily existence. Five to six thousand cooks were needed to cater to them. Vast
hoards of treasure were built up over the centuries to decorate the
palaces and to amuse the court. When the last dynasty fell the palaces
began to fall into disrepair. Some of the treasures were sold off by

former officials, some were lost in numerous fires, and large quantities were looted by the Japanese during the Sino-Japanese War. Thousands of crateloads of treasure were removed by Chiang Kai-shek's forces to Taiwan on the eve of the Communist takeover in 1949. However, some treasures still remain and give a notion of the former splendor of the imperial courts.

The Forbidden City and its palaces are slowly being renovated and considerable progress is being made in this work under the new regime. A visit will convince you that the Forbidden City is one of the most marvelous monuments to architecture in the world today.

The Forbidden City covers an area of about 250 acres and is surrounded by a wide moat and walls which are more than 35 feet high. There are towers built at each of the four corners of the Forbidden City, each with a pavilion on top. There are also four gates, each surmounted by a tower, giving entry to the city.

Apart from the central core of palaces (see plan: numbers 3–5 and 7–9) on your right, after entering through Tian An Men, is the Palace of Culture and the Imperial Library. In the southwest, or to the left, stands the former Imperial Printing House. In the northeast sector are the private palaces of Emperor Qian Long (1736–96), who was responsible for having the city almost entirely rebuilt, and the private palaces of Empress Ci Xi and the former apartments of the concubines. In the northwest sector are the former private apartments of the emperors and empresses. In the descriptions that follow we will confine ourselves mainly to the central core of palaces.

The Forbidden City has now been turned into a museum and contains a magnificent collection of Chinese bronzes, porcelain, paintings, jade, and other treasures. Here you will be able to see the famous jade suit and the "flying" horse (provided they are not out of the country on exhibition). The Forbidden City is open daily between 8:30 A.M. and 4:30 P.M., but note that tickets (costing 10 fen each) may be purchased up until 3:30 P.M. only and entry is not permitted after that time.

The First Courtyards

The central feature of the Forbidden City is the area harboring the six Imperial Palaces (three ceremonial and three private) set one behind the other along a north-south axis (numbers 3–5 and 7–9 on the plan). To reach the "central core" you must pass through the entrance tunnel of the Tian An Men Gate, then walk down a long roadway which leads to another gate called the Tuan Men. After passing this gate you will walk down an even longer corridor towards Wu Men, or the Meridian Gate, which gives entry to the grounds of the Inner Palaces.

The Meridian Gate (1) is the largest in the Forbidden City; it was built in 1420 and restored in 1647 and 1801. The five pavilions surmounting the gate are known as the "Five Phoenixes." It is from here that the emperor presided over military parades and ceremonies. Each year he would also announce the new calendar from the gate.

After you pass through the gateway you will come into a paved courtyard with the Jin Shui He, or Golden Water Stream, traversing it in a gentle arc from east to west. You cross the stream by one of the

THE FORBIDDEN CITY
(Entry courtyards not drawn to scale)

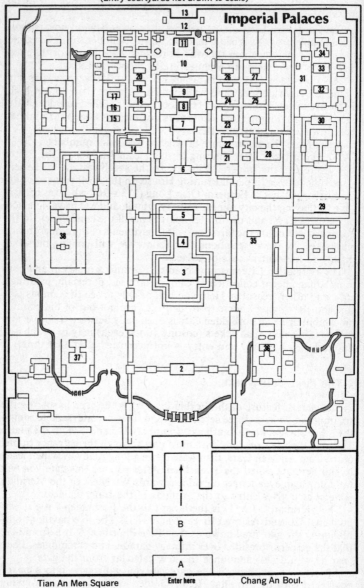

Imperial Palaces

Tian An Men Square   Enter here   Chang An Boul.

BEJING
BEIJING

five marble bridges believed to be symbols of the five virtues. Ahead stands the large Gate of Supreme Harmony (2), or Tai He Men. It is a two-roofed structure with orange glazed tiles and is seven bays wide. The building rests on a single tier surrounded by white marble balustrade; three sets of stairs lead to the terrace, the central one featuring a bas-relief carving in marble and used only by the emperor himself. Note the magnificent bronze lions guarding the entrance on either side, the bronze incense burners, and the model pavilion carved out of white marble and mounted on a small pedestal to the right of the stairways.

You are now about to enter the heart of the Forbidden City.

Three Ceremonial Palaces

After you pass through the gate you will enter an even larger courtyard, and in the distance before you, resting on a three-tiered terrace each surrounded by a white marble balustrade, is the Tai He Dian, or Hall of Supreme Harmony (3). As you walk towards it, note the three flights of stairs leading to the upper terrace: the middle one features a carved marble ramp over which the emperor was carried. There are many bronze incense burners flanking the stairways and, on the terrace, pairs of bronze storks and tortoises on either side. On the western side of the terrace there is a marble model of a pavilion housing a bronze grain measure; on the eastern side stands a sundial; these symbolize imperial justice and righteousness. Also note the two enormous bronze cauldrons with finely cast handles.

IMPERIAL PALACES—KEY

Entry through Tian An Men Gate (A) from Chang An Boul., then through Tuan Men (B) to:

The First Courtyards
1) Meridian Gate (Wu Men)
2) Gate of Supreme Harmony

The Three Ceremonial Palaces
3) Hall of Supreme Harmony
4) Hall of Perfect Harmony
5) Hall of the Preservation of Harmony
6) Gate of Heavenly Purity

The Three Private Palaces
7) Palace of Heavenly Purity
8) The Hall of Union
9) Palace of Earthly Tranquility

Imperial Garden and Outer Gates
10) Imperial Garden
11) Pavilion of Imperial Peace
12) Shun Zhen Men
13) Gate of Divine Pride

Northwest Sector
14) Palace of Culture of the Mind
15) Hall for Practicing Tai Ji Quan

16) Hall of Official Meetings
17) Palace of Eternal Spring
18) Hall of Assistance to Officials
19) Hall of Longevity
20) Palace of Accumulated Elegance

Northeast Sector
21) Palace of Abstinence
22) Hall of Sincerity and Solemnity
23) Hall of Charity
24) Hall for Carrying Out Imperial Orders
25) Hall of Eternal Peace
26) Hall of Time
27) Imperial Study
28) Hall for the Worship of Ancestors
29) Nine Dragon Screen
30) Palace of Peace and Longevity
31) Qian Long Garden
32) Hall for Cultivating Character
33) Hall of Happiness and Longevity
34) Pavilion of Peace and Harmony

Southeast Sector
35) Arrow Pavilion
36) Hall of Culture (Old Imperial Library)

Southwest Sector
37) Hall of Millitary Prowess
38) Garden of Peace and Tranquility

Inside the hall the central columns are gilded and carved with a dragon motif. There is a fine coffered ceiling. The emperor's throne stands on a raised platform surrounded by incense burners, screens, and other treasures. The emperor used the hall on great occasions to mark such events as the New Year, the nomination of military leaders, the publication of lists of scholars who had successfully passed the imperial examinations, the celebration of the winter solstice, and so on. All these ceremonies were performed amidst pomp and splendor.

Immediately behind this hall stands the Zhong He Dian, or Hall of Perfect Harmony (4), a small, square-shaped pavilion with a single roof; there are traditional Chinese windows on all sides. Inside there is a raised throne, a sedan chair on either side, and a fine array of incense burners, room heaters, and decorative treasures; the ceiling is beautifully crafted. It is here that the emperor would come to make final preparations before presiding over the ceremonies in the Hall of Supreme Harmony.

The next palace is the Hall of the Preservation of Harmony (5), or Bao He Dian. It is a two-roofed pavilion, seven bays wide, housing a large throne. The emperor used to preside over ceremonies here: receiving the scholars who had passed the court examinations and, under the Qing, hosting enormous banquets in honor of foreign emissaries and ambassadors.

There are three sets of stairs leading to the front of the throne and two sets leading to the side. Note the four incense burners standing before the throne and the two gilt lamps. The hall is now often used to house exhibits of some of China's art treasures, the most recent being the collection of bronze figurines, chariots, and horses taken from the eastern Han tomb in Wuwei (Gansu Province) in 1969. There is also a permanent exhibition of Chinese art objects inside the hall.

You now descend the steps from the three-tiered terrace into a courtyard and walk toward the Gate of Heavenly Purity (6), or Qian Qing Men. It has three sets of stairs, the middle one with the traditional carved marble ramp, guarded by two gilt lions; on either side stand two giant bronze cauldrons. This gateway leads to the three private palaces or apartments, as distinct from the first three, which were used for ceremonial purposes.

Three Private Palaces

After passing through the gateway you will enter another courtyard where a wide path lined with a white marble balustrade leads to the Palace of Heavenly Purity (7), or Qian Qing Gong. Note the four large bronze incense burners on the terrace. The palace has a two-tiered roof featuring fine sets of figurines on the roof line corners. Note the inscription in Chinese and Mongolian on the framed plaque between the eaves of the roof; also the bronze grain measure to the left and the sundial to the right (again symbols of imperial justice and righteousness); and the bronze cranes and tortoises standing on either side of the terrace (symbols of immortality). Walk to the end of the terrace and you will see, at either end, a gilded model pavilion standing on a white three-tiered stone terrace. The purpose of these models is not understood.

The palace once contained the emperor's bedroom, but later, under the Qing, it was used by the emperor as an audience room and for receptions. Four incense burners stand before the throne; there are three sets of stairs mounting the throne dais in front and two on the sides. Note the candle holders in the form of storks and the very ornate dragon screen behind the throne. There are huge framed mirrors to the right and left of the throne. Note also the cupboard on the left with the fine woodwork. The carved ceiling is magnificent.

Behind this hall is Jiao Tai Dian, or the Hall of Union (8), a single-roofed square pavilion with inscription over the entrance doorway in Chinese and Mongolian. Within there is a small throne surrounded on all sides by caskets with covers on, housing the imperial seals. Over-head is a fine ceiling with a recessed portion featuring a coiled gilt dragon. On the left-hand side of the throne is an enormous clock built for Qian Long in the eighteenth century, on the right-hand side a model of a two-roofed pavilion housing three bronze vessels emptying into each other. There is also a tiny bronze figure reading a gold tablet and seated on a small wooden dais.

To the rear of this hall is the Palace of Earthly Tranquility (9), or Kun Ning Gong. This palace, now closed, was variously used as a residence for the empresses under the Ming, a venue for the sacrifices to the God of the Kitchen, and a nuptial chamber for the last Qing emperor and his bride.

Imperial Garden and Outer Gates

By descending the stairs of the terrace at the rear and passing through Kun Ning Man, or Gate of Earthly Tranquility, you can enter the Imperial Garden (10), or Yu Hua Yuan. This is a quiet place where you may wish to sit for a while and take a rest after your long walk. There are a number of fine old trees in the gardens; particularly note-worthy are the two intertwined around each other and known locally as the "love trees." On leaving the garden you pass through the Sun Zhen Gate (12), and walk towards the massive outer Gate of Divine Pride (13). You have now completed your tour of the Inner Palaces of the Forbidden City.

Other Palaces

You will find that it takes a few hours to stroll through the Inner Palaces and surrounding courtyards, but, should you wish to continue, there are many other palaces to see. If you are too tired you could arrange with your guide to come back on another day. Most people do not have enough time and find the tour of the Inner Palaces to be sufficient.

The outer palaces are not described in this book, but the following list is indicative of what you should cover if you wish to take a more extensive tour of the Forbidden City. As there are sometimes special exhibitions held in the "outer" halls and pavilions, you should ask your guide for details.

In the northwest sector: the Palace of Culture of the Mind (14), or Yang Xin Dian, and the Six Western Palaces (15–20).

In the northeast sector: The Palace of Abstinence (21), or Zhai Gong; the six Eastern Palaces; the Hall of Worship of Ancestors (28), or Feng Xian Dian; the Palace of Peace and Longevity (3), or Ning Shou Gong, and the Annexes. The passageway to the Palace of Peace and Longevity features a magnificent Nine Dragon Screen (29) which rivals the one in Bei Hai Park.

In the southeast sector: the Palace of Culture (36), or Wen Hua Dian, where the Imperial Library was housed.

TEMPLE OF HEAVEN

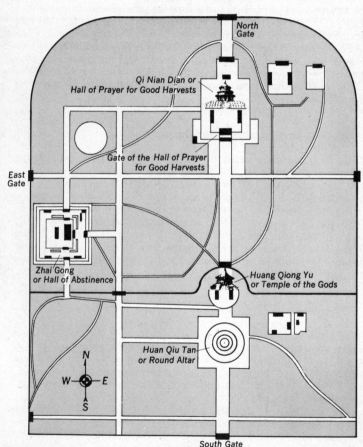

North Gate

Qi Nian Dian or Hall of Prayer for Good Harvests

Gate of the Hall of Prayer for Good Harvests

East Gate

Zhai Gong or Hall of Abstinence

Huang Qiong Yu or Temple of the Gods

Huan Qiu Tan or Round Altar

N W E S

South Gate

Temple of Heaven

The Temple of Heaven is the most famous temple in China and should be given high priority during your visit. The name Temple of Heaven, or Tian Tan, actually refers to a group of ceremonial buildings inside a walled park in southeast Peking. They were built in the fifteenth century, restored in the eighteenth century under Qian Long, and in this century under the Communist government.

The most important building in the grounds is the Qi Nian Dian, or Hall of Prayer for Good Harvest (sometimes known as the Temple of Annual Prayer), where the emperor would go each year to spend the night fasting and in prayer. The temple is set on a triple marble terrace, each with a balustrade. The terraces are intersected by eight flights of stairs, the major one set with a carved ramp of white marble. The temple is round with three roofs of glazed blue tiles, the top roof being surmounted by a gilded ball. The temple is 123 feet high and (apart from the roof tiles) is constructed entirely of wood without any nails being used. The absence of nails makes the temple one of the architectural wonders of the world. The exterior of the building is decorated lavishly in red, blue, and green with elaborate gilt overlay.

The temple has but one door which opens to the south. Inside there are 24 wooden columns arranged in a double circle around four central ones. All of these are made from the trunks of trees brought from the south of China. The four central columns are said to represent the four seasons of the year, the outer circle of twelve the months of the year, and the inner circle of twelve the hours of the day (according to the old Chinese calendar). All these columns support an elaborate system of pillars that hold up the three roofs, an arrangement that has attracted the admiration of architects throughout the ages.

The temple is flanked on either side by two blue-roofed pavilions with exterior walls decorated in red and gold. These pavilions have an elegance that blends perfectly with the style of the temple itself. Opposite the temple is the Gate of the Prayer for Good Harvests, or Qi Nian Men. You pass through this double gate and walk along a wide pathway through another gate to a round-walled enclosure housing the Temple of the Gods, or Huang Qiong Yu. It is a small circular temple built entirely of wood, with a conical blue-tiled roof capped with a gilt ball; it dates from 1530. Here you can amuse yourself by standing close to the inside of the circular wall and whispering a message. Listen and your voice will come back along the wall from the opposite direction. There are also the San Yin Shi, or Three Echo Stones, from which you can create unusual acoustic effects (ask your guide to demonstrate).

A little farther south of this temple is the Huan Qiu Tan, or Round Altar. It is here that the emperor would come to make a sacrifice to heaven. The ceremony was accompanied by the chanting of priests, burning of incense, banging of gongs, and the performance of ritual music. This ceremony was one of the most important of the year, the Chinese believing that the very destiny of the whole nation depended upon this mysterious rite. The Round Altar comprises three terraces in tiers one above the other, each surrounded by a white marble balustrade with 360 pillars. The terraces were thought to represent man, earth, and heaven.

When the "Son of Heaven" went from the Forbidden City to the grounds of the Temple of Heaven to perform ceremonies throughout the year, all windows and gates along the way had to be closed, no noise was permitted, and no foreigner allowed to set eyes on the procession. Only the emperor himself, the princes of the court, priests, officials, musicians, and soldiers guarding the procession were allowed to take part.

The Great Wall

The Chinese name for the Great Wall is Wan Li Chang Cheng, or "the Long Wall of Ten Thousand Li." The first sections were built as early as the fifth century B.C. when a number of Chinese states in the north were fighting against each other and occasionally against the northern "barbarian." It was not until the unification of the empire under Qin Shi Huang Di in B.C. 221 that the various sections of the Wall were linked up. It is said that more than 300,000 men worked for ten years to complete it. The wall had a pounded earth interior with stone facing walls and stone roadway along the top. It was built wide enough to allow a brace of five horses to gallop between the battlements and was thus used to convey soldiers, arms, and food with great speed to various parts of the northern frontier.

From the sixth century to the fourteenth the wall was abandoned and fell into disuse, but after the Mongols took China and were repulsed eventually by the Ming in 1368, the emperor decided to rebuild the wall. The rebuilding and restoration continued up until the sixteenth century. However, when the Manchu armies captured China and the Qing Dynasty ruled (1644–1911), the wall was again abandoned and fell into ruin.

It has now been restored at three famous passes and you may visit one of them, Ba Da Ling, about 40 miles from Peking.

You may travel with your guide by car to Ba Da Ling or go by train. You should set aside a full day for the car journey, leaving at about 8–8:30 A.M. in the morning so that you will have time to take in the Ming Tombs on the return journey in the afternoon. This program would normally get you back to your hotel around 4 P.M. If you go by car you should ask your guide to stop at the old gate which lies to the right hand side of the road at a point where you begin to climb the foothills. The gate is built of white marble and inside there are bas-relief carvings of Buddhist themes with inscriptions in Chinese, Mongol, Sanskrit, Tibetan, Uighur, and Tangut. The carvings are thought to date from the fourteenth century and are rare examples.

You may also visit the Ba Da Ling section of the Great Wall by train. You will find the journey pleasant, the compartment comfortable and well ventilated, and the scenery interesting. The history and details of the structure of the 3,000-mile wall are provided in Chinese, English, and Japanese on the radio in your compartment. Many visitors are finding this to be the most convenient and comfortable method of visiting the Great Wall. However, if you do go by train you will have to visit the Ming Tombs another day.

Whatever way you travel to the Great Wall, always wear comfortable shoes with nonslip soles. The climb is steep in parts and sometimes the stones are slippery. If you are going in cooler weather wear plenty of warm clothes; the wind that comes through the mountain in that region will cut right through you.

Everybody who visits Beijing wants to see the Great Wall and for a good reason: it is one of the wonders of the world. As you stand on the top tower and look at the wall snaking its way across the tops of the mountains, close your eyes for a moment. See in your mind's eye the ancient armies locked in combat, and hear the whistle of arrows and the clang of striking swords.

It is a place to reflect upon the past and wonder about the future.

The Ming Tombs

For almost 3,000 years Chinese rulers have had tombs built on the outskirts of their capital. The Zhou emperors appear to be the first who adopted this practice—at least, no earlier tombs have been found—and the tradition was maintained throughout the ages right down to the Qing.

The earliest Ming Tomb, located outside Nanjing, is that of Hong Wu, the founder of the Ming Dynasty. The second Ming emperor reigned only for four years before he was overthrown by Yong Le in 1403, who then moved the capital to Beijing. During the third emperor's reign the site for his tomb was selected outside Beijing using the age-old method of geomancy, which takes into account the disposition of wind and water (*feng shui*) at the site. The foothills and mountains protect the corpse of the emperor from the evil spirits carried by the northern wind, and the lower sloping ground was ideal for the gentle flow of water before the tomb.

When you visit the area you will be impressed by the beauty of the location and the tranquility of the surroundings. It is now a favorite picnic spot for foreign residents in Beijing, and if you go there on a weekend you will find many families sitting on the grass under the old pine trees that dot the grounds.

The Chinese name for the area is Shi San Ling, or "the Thirteen Tombs"; thirteen of the sixteen Ming emperors are buried there. Only two of the sites have been restored, and of these, only one has been excavated. Both are worth visiting, but you may not have time if you are going to the Great Wall and the Ming Tombs the same day. If you are not pressed for time, you can visit both comfortably and even ask your guide to take you to some of the other tombs scattered in the hills. They are suffering extreme deterioration, with splintered timbers, grass growing on the roofs, tiles spilled throughout the area, statues broken, and pillars overturned. One thing to keep in mind if you are going without a guide: you are not allowed to cut across country on foot to a neighboring tomb, but must go back along the road by car and then proceed to the other tomb.

The site where the tomb buildings have been renovated and the tomb itself excavated is Ding Ling, which is the tomb of the fourteenth emperor, Wan Li (1573–1620). The site that has not been excavated but where the buildings have been renovated is the tomb of the third Ming emperor, Yung Le (1403–1424), the first emperor to be buried in the area. Both sites will be described; but first, details of the famous route leading to the tomb area will be given.

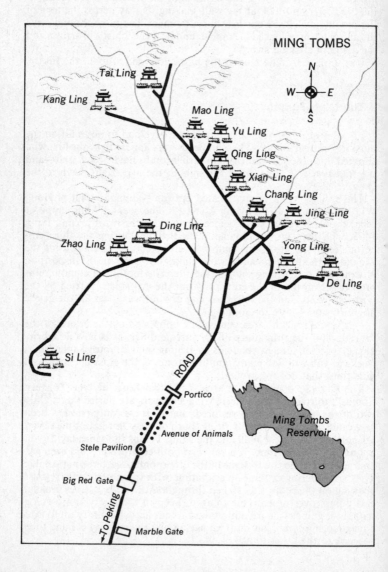

The "Sacred Way"

As you begin to approach the site by car, the first sign of the tomb area is a white marble portico with five gateways located off the road to the right. It was once the entry point of the Sacred Way. Note the fine bas-relief carvings forming the base of the pillars. The portico was built in 1540.

A little further on you will come to the Da Hong Men, or Big Red Gate, which is a massive edifice about 120 feet high. There are three gateways: the two on either side were used by the living rulers, and the central gateway was used only to carry the corpse of the dead emperor into the sacred area. This huge gateway was once part of a wall which enclosed the area. No one was allowed to enter under pain of death, except of course the officials and attendants who resided there permanently, nor was anyone allowed to enter on horseback.

After passing down the avenue a short way you will come to a twin-roofed pavilion with a single archway in each side leading to an open inner chamber housing a stele. This is the Pei Ting, or Stele Pavilion. The stele is about 30 feet high and stands on the back of a giant tortoise about 6 feet high. There is an inscription on one face of the stele by the fourth Ming emperor and on the other by the fourth Qing emperor, the famous Qian Long. Outside at each of the four corners of the building stands a large marble column with a dragon carved in bas-relief around its length and a mythical beast perched on top.

A few hundred yards further the famous Avenue of Animals begins. Stone animals had first been placed before tombs during the reign of the Han (B.C. 206–A.D. 220), and the custom was adopted by the rulers of all the dynasties that followed. At the Ming Tomb site there is a row of animals on either side of the road, one pair being spaced equidistant from the next pair along the route. There are six animals represented in all: a lion, a mythical animal called the *xie chi,* a camel, an elephant, another mythical beast called a *qi lin,* and a horse. Each animal is shown in a standing and a kneeling position. In all, there are 12 statues on each side of the road, a total of 24.

In accordance with the traditions of geomancy, the Sacred Way turns slightly to the right, and reveals a row of human statues dating from the fifteenth century on either side of the road. First there are two military mandarins with swords, next two civilian mandarins holding tablets, and finally two retired mandarins. The exact significance of the statues is not clear, but they are thought to have been erected in order to serve the dead emperor and his wives in the next world.

Beyond the Avenue of Animals stands a very small portico with three gates, the road passing on either side of it toward the sites of the thirteen tombs.

Tomb of Emperor Wan Li

You will first come to a small bridge with a balustrade leading to an unmarked stele standing on the back of a stone tortoise. The road then leads to an entrance gate with three arched doorways set in the wall. This is the entrance to the Ding Ling, or Tomb of Emperor Wan Li (1573–1620).

After entering the sacred area you walk along a wide path toward a terrace which is intersected on either side by a red colored wall surmounted by glazed yellow tiles. All that remains of the building that once stood on the terrace are the bases of a number of stone columns. There are three stairways leading from the terrace to a courtyard with many old trees growing on either side. Ahead there are three stairways, the middle one with a bas-relief slab ramp, leading up to a terrace which was the foundation of a building known as the Ling En Dian, a place where sacrifices were made. The bases of twenty columns are all that remain of this building.

You then continue along the path and pass through a gateway leading to a large square tower (Fang Cheng) surmounted by a pavilion housing a stele. The tower forms part of the wall that encircles the tumulus. At the foot of the tower there is a stone altar with two stone vessels standing on either side of a larger sacrificial vessel. To the right and left are two small buildings housing a museum of the site.

Steps at the side of the tower lead up to the chamber housing the stele. The tablet rests on a tiered base carved out of marble.

To enter the excavated tomb you must go down the three flights of stairs set into the tumulus. The first chamber is modern and of no particular interest, but the marble gateway leading from it to the next chamber contained two six-inch-thick marble doors which are now on display behind glass. Note the "locking stone" standing against the wall; this fitted into a slot in the floor and would slide down to lock the door from the inside once it had been closed. Another pair of stone doors lead to the central chamber where there are three altars standing in a row, the first two being those of the empresses and the third that of the emperor. The vessel which stands on a pedestal in front of the altars was filled with oil at the time of burial to provide an "eternal" flame. Behind this lamp are five pedestals used to support ritual vessels (these are missing); behind them is a throne with a finely carved dragon on the back. Marble pedestals stand on either side of each altar.

Another doorway leads into the last chamber, which is larger than the others and features a stone base where the coffins of the emperor and the empresses were placed. Copies of the treasure chest are in position on the dais.

There are two side chambers leading off the central one, each containing a dais, but they were found to be empty when the excavations were made.

If you have time you should try to visit the two small museums located on either side of the pathway leading towards the exit.

Tomb of Emperor Yong Le

Yong Le was the first Ming emperor to be buried in the sacred area (1424). His remains along with those of his wife lie within the huge unexcavated tumulus.

Entry to the sacred area is through three huge doorways set into a vast gate which is part of the wall enclosing the grounds and tomb. Inside, to the right of the courtyard, is a twin-roofed pavilion enclosing a Qing stele mounted on a mythical scaled beast that looks like an overfed dragon. There is a fine coffered ceiling.

At the end of the first courtyard stands the Gate of Eminent Favors, or Ling En Men, with three doorways and a single roof of yellow glazed tiles. As you pass down the stairway on the other side of the gate, note the center ramp in white marble with figures in bas-relief: a coiled dragon, clouds encircling mountains, horses in fields. Note also to the right and left the model pavilion with a wall of glazed tiles; the low roof presents an ideal opportunity to photograph the roof figurines.

At the end of the long courtyard with large pine trees dotted on either side stands the Ling En Dian, or Hall of Eminent Favors, a twin-roofed building on a three-tiered white marble terrace with balustrades all around. Three sets of stairs lead up to the building, the central stairway with a marble ramp depicting the same motif as before but in a slightly different design. Inside the hall, 32 giant columns made from single tree trunks (from South China) supported the roof by means of enormous cross beams. There is a fine coffered ceiling. On the opposite side of the hall there is a screen wall hiding the exit from view.

When you leave this building note the two magnificent pine trees to the left of the path. Immediately ahead is another gate with three doorways leading to a final large courtyard. The path leads through a small portico past some beautiful trees on either side to a sacrificial altar with five ritual vessels. Behind is the Fang Cheng, or Square Tower, with the Ming Lou pavilion on top. There is a tunnel sloping upwards through the Square Tower leading to the pavilion housing the stele and the tumulus. The tumulus has not been excavated, and its probable contents have aroused the curiosity of archeologists around the world.

Summer Palace

The Summer Palace is a fine place to go if you want to relax. There is a large lake where you can hire a rowboat in the summer or skate in winter. There is also an excellent restaurant, the Ting Li Guan, or Pavilion for Listening to Birds Sing. If you feel energetic or wish to walk off a large lunch, you can climb the many stairs to the top of the man-made Hill of Longevity. Or you can just sit under the shade of a tree. The Summer Palace is only 45 minutes' comfortable drive from the heart of Beijing.

The first palace known to have existed on the site was built in the twelfth century. At that stage the lake was not very extensive; it was considerably enlarged under the Yuan in the fourteenth century. Other temples and pavilions were built there under the Ming, and the site was developed enormously under Emperor Qian Long (1736–1796) of the Qing.

The area became known as the Summer Palace, because all the court stayed there during summer to avoid the heat of Beijing. The palaces and pavilions were burned down by the Anglo-French allied force in

1860, and the place fell into ruins. In 1888, Empress Dowager Ci Xi (or Tzu Hsi) had it rebuilt with large sums of money earmarked for expanding the Chinese navy. The marble boat constructed under her reign, which now sits on the edge of the lake, therefore has certain ironic significance. It was the Empress Dowager who renamed the area the Yi He Yuan. The palace was seriously damaged again in 1900 during the Boxer Rebellion but was restored once again in 1903. Three-quarters of the 660 acres that make up the area is occupied by Lake Kun Ming, the remaining quarter being taken up by Longevity Hill and the foreshores.

The major attractions (in approximate order when walking from the eastern entrance around the northern foreshore) are the Eastern Palaces Gate or Dong Gon Men, the Benevolence and Longevity Palace or Ren Shou Dian, the Palace of Virtue and Harmony or De He Yuan, the Jade Waves Palace or Yu Lan Tang, the Palace of Joy and Longevity or Le Shou Tang, the Palace of Orderly Clouds of Pia Yun Dian.

Still proceeding along the foreshore you will come to one of the most interesting features of the Summer Palace—a covered way with beams painted to depict historical and fictional events and landscapes of Hangzhou. This leads past the Ting Li Guan Restaurant, located in a pavilion on the right, and goes on to the "stone boat."

Returning along the covered way to the Palace of Orderly Clouds you may, if you have time, climb the many sets of stairs to see the Bronze Kiosk or Tong Ting, the Pavilion of Precious Clouds or Bao Yun Ge, and the Hall of the Sea of Wisdom or Zhi Hui Hai.

By returning to the northern shore and following the shoreline as it turns south you will be able to walk to the elegant arched bridge which leads out to a small islet called the Temple of the Dragon King. Just before reaching the bridge you will pass the Bronze Ox protected by a stone balustrade. On your way south along the eastern shore you will pass the place where rowboats are hired.

If you have sufficient time, you may visit the ruins of the Old Summer Palace, located only a few miles from the existing Summer Palace. Nothing much remains now except a few blocks of stone and broken marble that once belonged to the European palaces constructed under Qian Long between 1740 and 1747.

The old Summer Palace, or Yuan Ming Yuan, was once a sumptuous and magnificent pleasure ground for the court. Hundreds of palaces dotted the area. Superb landscaping was created; exotic flowers and trees adorned the slopes, huge pleasure-boats plied the lakes and streams. The emperor's apartments were adorned with art treasures of an astonishing richness.

The British and French troops took the area in 1860, set aside the most valuable objects for Queen Victoria and Napoleon III, looted the remainder, and set fire to all the palaces. Although an attempt was made to restore them about twenty years later, it was unsuccessful, and they fell completely into ruin.

The area is a favorite picnic spot for foreign residents. It is also a pleasant place to spend a quiet hour.

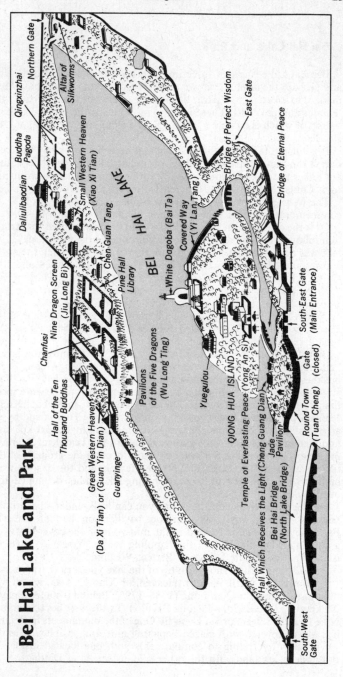

Bei Hai Lake and Park

Northern Gate

Qingxinzhai

Buddha Pagoda

Daiiulibaodian

Altar of Silkworms

Bridge of Perfect Wisdom

East Gate

Small Western Heaven (Xiao Xi Tian)

Chanfusi

Nine Dragon Screen (Jiu Long Bi)

Chen Guan Tang

Bridge of Eternal Peace

Pine Hall Library

BEI HAI LAKE

Covered Way (Yi Lan Tang)

Hall of the Ten Thousand Buddhas

White Dagoba (Bai Ta)

Great Western Heaven (Da Xi Tian) or (Guan Yin Dian)

Pavilions of the Five Dragons (Wu Long Ting)

Guanyinge

Yuegulou

QIONG HUA ISLAND

South-East Gate (Main Entrance)

Temple of Everlasting Peace (Yong An Si)

Round Town (Tuan Cheng)

Gate (closed)

Hall Which Receives the Light (Cheng Guang Dian)

Jade Pavilion

Bei Hai Bridge (North Lake Bridge)

South-West Gate

Bei Hai Lake and Park

Bei Hai Lake is one of three imperial lakes in the center of Beijing and perhaps the most attractive of all. The shores of the lake have been made into an attractive park, beautifully landscaped and dotted with temples and pavilions. There is an island close to the southeast shore on top of which is a famous landmark in Beijing: the white dagoba, or Bai Ta.

It is known that a pleasure palace had been built there by the Liao over a thousand years ago and that the first lake on the site was dug out under the Jin some time in the twelfth century. When the Mongols took China, Kubilai Khan decided to live on the island in the lake.

The White Dagoba was built by Emperor Shun Zhi in 1651 to commemorate the first visit to Beijing of the Dalai Lama of Tibet.

Over the centuries the park and lake went through periods of restoration followed by periods of neglect, right up until the present day. The lake was deepened in 1951 and the marble bridge separating the north and middle lake constructed in 1956. The park was closed after the Cultural Revolution in 1966 and reopened again only in March 1978.

If you go in by the southeast gate, which is the main entrance, you will note the large curved wall on your left. This is the Round Town, or Tuan Cheng, which was once an island in the lake. The walls of the Tower, built in 1417, protected the residence of Kubilai Khan. Although parts of the wall date from the fifteenth century, the buildings within date from the middle of the eighteenth. The most important building is the Hall Which Receives the Light, or Cheng Guang Dian, but there is a smaller building worth visiting called the Jade Pavilion. It was built in 1745 to house a black jade bowl said to measure more than 15 feet in circumference. The bowl was a gift to Kubilai Khan.

From the Round Town you may cross to Qiong Hua Island by an arched marble bridge which curves gently to the right, the path passing under an archway with three gateways toward the Temple of Everlasting Peace, or Yong An Si. You can walk through the grounds of the temple to the White Dagoba. Both the temple and the dagoba were built in 1651. The view of the surrounding lake and of Beijing itself is outstanding.

On the northern side of the island you can walk under a beautifully restored "covered way" past numerous pavilions on the shoreline. The Fangshan restaurant is located at the mid-point of the covered way in a building called the Hall of the Rippling Waves. You may leave the island by crossing the Bridge of Perfect Wisdom.

As you approach the northern tip of the lake you turn sharply to the left towards the Small Western Heaven, or Xiao Xi Tian, which was built under Emperor Qian Long (1736–1796). Behind it stands a pavilion known as the Buddha Pagoda Pavilion. To the west lies the famous Nine Dragon Screen, or Jiu Long Bi. One of the monuments in Beijing, it is a wall covered with glazed depicting nine dragons playing in the waves. It is interesting to compare this with one located inside the Forbidden City (and with the other famous screen at Datong).

Further to the west on the shore of the lake there are attractive pavilions called the Wu Long Ting, or Pavilions of the Five Dragons, built in memory of five brothers who were famous scholars in the second century B.C.

Still further west and against the far wall of the park are the buildings known as Great West Heaven (Daxidian, Guan Yin Dian), first erected under Emperor Kang Xi (1662–1723). From here you can stroll along the western edge of the lake to the southwest gate.

Jing Shan, or Coal Hill Park

Jing Shan Park, otherwise known as Coal Hill or Mei Shan, is due north of the Forbidden City. It is simple to locate and easily recognized by the symmetrical layout of the five pavilions on the hill, the largest one being at the top.

The main entrance gate is through the southern wall directly opposite the Gate of Divine Pride (Shen Wu Men) of the Forbidden City. On entering you will see before you the Beautiful View Tower, or Qi Wang Lou. The path leads up the hillside to the top of the central hill where the Pavilion of Ten Thousand Springs, or Wan Chun Ting, stands. Here you may take in the magnificent panorama of Beijing.

The park was used by the court from the thirteenth century onwards. Under the Ming, five man-made hills were constructed, supposedly by using earth taken from the moat around the Imperial City. In the time of the Qing, Qian Long (1736–1796) had pavilions built, trees planted, and the park stocked with animals. The park fell into disuse in the nineteenth and twentieth centuries but has recently been restored. It was closed during the Cultural Revolution and only reopened in 1978.

There are two stories connected with the park. One claims that an emperor had coal buried under the central hill, hence the name often given to the park. The other alleges that the last Ming emperor hanged himself there in 1644. The first story is uncorroborated by evidence; but the second may be true, there being some historic documents which tend to confirm the event.

Drum Tower

The Drum Tower, or Gu Lou, is one of the oldest buildings in Beijing. It is located due north of Coal Hill at the northern end of Di An Men Dajie, and lies on a north-south axis, passing through the Forbidden City and Tian An Men Square. The present building is over 700 years old, having been erected under the Ming in 1420. It was restored under the Qing. The site marks what was once the center of the old Mongol capital Da Du, founded in the thirteenth century.

The tower has a solid brick base intersected in the north-south direction by three passageways and in a east-west direction by one passageway. Above the base is a pavilion with a balcony and a triple roof.

Drums used to be beaten from the tower at sunset every day.

Bell Tower

The Bell Tower is located due north of the Drum Tower. It was first constructed under the Ming but was later burned down. The present building, comprising a base (with straighter sides than the Drum Tower) and an upper story with a double roof of gray tiles, was constructed under the reign of Qian Long (1736–1796). The upper story is traversed by three passageways from each side. It once housed a giant iron bell but this has been removed.

There is a legend that the virgin daughter of the bellmaker threw herself into the molten iron before the bell was cast. Her father was only able to grab her shoe as she plunged into the vat, and legend has it that the bell when struck made a soft sound resembling the sound of the Chinese word for shoe *(xie)*.

Lama Temple

The temple lies at the northern end of Dongsi Street in the northeastern sector of Beijing, near the Temple of Confucius and the Guo Zi Jian. Known in Chinese as the Yong He Gong, or Palace of Peace and Harmony, it was at one time the palace of the prince who later became emperor. According to the custom of the time, it was then declared forbidden ground, but nine years after his son, Qian Long, ascended the throne (1745), it was made into a lamasery devoted to the cult of the living lama.

The monastery housed many hundreds of Tibetan lamas and disciples who studied there. Sacred Tibetan texts were chanted from the walls each day, and on certain occasions the famous Devil Dance was performed. A doll made of dough and stuffed with artificial blood was torn to pieces during the ritual by the priests. In the earliest forms of the ritual human sacrifices were made.

The first courtyard leads toward the Tianwangdian, or Hall of the Celestial Guardians; here there is a statue of the Maitreya Buddha flanked by his celestial guardians. The defender of Buddhism, Weituo, faces north behind the screen. In the second courtyard there is a large stone pond supporting a bronze representation of Xumi Mountain which, according to Buddhist doctrine is the "king of mountains" and the center of the world. The founder of Buddhism, Sakyamuni, lives at the peak in paradise, represented by the altar at the top of the bronze.

In the galleries on either side are many figures of Congkaba (in yellow cap), the founder of this particular lamaist sect. On the northern end of the courtyard stands the Hall of Eternal Harmony, or Yonghedian, housing statues of the buddha surrounded by disciples, called *Buohan*.

After the third courtyard stands the Yongyoudian, or Hall of Eternal Protection; then beyond the fourth courtyard, is the Falundian, or Hall of the Wheel of Dharma (i.e. Law). In this last pavilion there is a 10-meter-high bronze image of Congkaba sitting cross-legged on a raised pedestal, hands clasped together. Both the Dalai and Panchan lamas were his disciples. The tiny statue of the buddha seated in front of the large figure is the most venerated of all those in the lamasery.

The frescoes on the walls of this temple illustrate the life of the sect's founder.

In the gallery off the fourth courtyard, in the Hall of the Mi Sect, some of the erotic statues are to be found, e.g., the Duola warrior attendant possessing a human body but with a beast's head who is copulating with a beautiful woman.

At the far end of the fifth courtyard stands the Wanfuge, or Pavilion of Ten Thousand Happinesses, a triple-roof structure housing the giant standing image of the Maitreya Buddha in his Tibetan form. It was carved out of a single piece of white sandalwood, stands 18 meters high, and has a girth of 3 meters.

The Yonghe Gong is just a few minutes' drive from the Jianguo, Great Wall (Chang Cheng), and Huadu Hotels. Public buses 116 (most direct), 44, or 13 will also get you there.

Temple of the White Cypress Grove

This temple, known as Bailinsi in Chinese, lies just a short distance to the southeast of the Lama Temple. It was founded in 1347, under the Mongols, and served as a retreat for monks studying the sutras, but is now used for other purposes.

Temple of the White Dagoba

The first pagoda built on the site was erected in the eleventh century. Kubilai Khan had it opened up in 1272 and hundreds of relics were found. It was then restored and a Lamaist Temple built in front of it. The temple was rebuilt under the Ming and restored under the early Qing. When repairs were made in 1978, archeologists found several boxes containing over twenty relics: a small buddha (118.2 g) made of pure gold encrusted with 44 gems; a small glazed Goddess of Mercy; a gilded bronze box containing 33 fragments of buddhist relics; a monk's cap and kasaya (made of appliquéd brocade); and a Tripitaka sutra in the handwriting of Emperor Dian Long (offered to the temple in 1753). According to buddhist practice, all dagobas had three treasures hidden within to keep away evil spirits: a statue, the scriptures, and a monk's kasaya and cap. All these objects are on display in the White Dagoba (*Baidasi*).

The Dagoba is located in the northwest sector of Beijing on the northern side of Fu Cheng Men, down a little lane that must be traversed on foot.

Great Bell Temple

Located not far from the corner of Baishiqiao Road and the North Circular Road, the temple, known as Dazhongsi in Chinese, houses an enormous bell. The bell was cast by Yao Guangxiao under orders from the Ming emperor, Yong Le (reigned 1403–24). It weighs 46.5 tons, measures 22 feet high, 10 feet across; and is 8 inches at the thickest part of its wall. There are 17 buddhist sutras inscribed on its sides, written in 220,000 characters by Ming calligrapher Shen Du. There are complete passages of the Diamond and Lotus sutras inscribed.

The bell was cast in a pit, scores of furnaces being used to pour the molten bronze through a great many clay troughs branching off in a multitude of directions. The bell had to be cast in one pouring and is testimony to the superb skill of the Ming craftsmen. However, the bell lay in its pit for 170 years before another Ming emperor, Shen Zong, had it moved to the Temple of Longevity in 1577. When the temple collapsed in 1743, the bell was moved to its present site, then called Jueshengsi. From then on the temple became known by its present name.

A number of bells cast under the Song, Yuan, Ming, and Qing Dynasties—a period spanning almost a thousand years—are on display in a courtyard of the temple grounds. Although the bell is more than 570 years old, it gives a full sonorous vibration when struck, and can be heard, it is said, over 25 miles away. The bell resonates for over a minute when struck.

Yellow Temple

The remains of the Huangsi, as it is called in Chinese, have been restored. The temple, located just off the North Circular Road after the Changpinglu crossroad—you will identify it by the gold and white dagoba—has existed on the site since the Liao. In the seventeenth century, part of the temple was made into a residence for visiting Panchen Lamas from Tibet. When one of them died in residence in the reign of Qian Long (1736–1796), the emperor had a white marble mausoleum built to house the remains of the visiting dignitary.

Temple of the Five Pagodas

The Temple of the Five Pagodas, or Wu Ta Si, is not easy to find; it is tucked away behind the zoo in the middle of a field on the outskirts of Beijing. To get to the temple you should head north along the Bai Shi Qiao Road, which passes between the Zi Zhu Yuan (Purple Bamboo) Park on the left-hand side and the Beijing Zoo on the right. About half a mile along this road you will cross a stream. The dirt track which follows the stream to the east leads to the temple. The temple is not Chinese in style at all, but Indian; it was constructed in 1473 from a model of an Indian Buddhist temple presented to the Ming Court of Yong Le. The five pagodas arising from the base are more like obelisks with numerous horizontal platforms diminishing in width towards the apex.

Temple of the Big Buddha

The Dafosi, as it is known in Chinese, is located opposite the Institute of Minorities, just off Baishiqiao Road. All that remains of the temple is the twin-roofed central pavilion, but this can only be seen from fields on the western side, as the site now forms part of a housing complex. The temple was founded in the early sixteenth century. It used to contain a huge statue of the Buddha in polychrome wood, hence the name given to the temple. It is not certain whether the statue is still within the pavilion.

Beijing "Atmosphere"

There are many places not far from your hotel that convey an idea of local life. These streets are dusty, noisy, and full of people, bicycles, tripeds, and carts. They are not tourist places but simply areas of Beijing where the locals are going about their daily business.

If there has been any conscious selection in the areas described below it relates to shopping: in all these locations you can shop as the Chinese do, in small stores crammed full of merchandise.

One of the busiest quarters in Beijing is the area around Qian Men Street, which runs directly south from the Qian Men Gate at the southern edge of Tian An Men Square. Here you can mix with the crowds, visit the busy Chinese shops, and wander down the tiny *hutung* or lanes which crisscross the back areas.

You are also close to Liu Li Chang, which is an interesting area to visit whether or not you wish to visit the antique shops there.

Another region to visit for local flavor is the area around Qongwenmen Street, which cuts across Chang An Jie a few blocks east of the Beijing Hotel. Both the north and south sides of the street are interesting. If you take the south side you can stop in at the "Theater Shop" to hunt for antiques. When walking south from Chang An Jie it is on the left-hand side (No. 12) only a short distance from the intersection.

Then of course there is Wang Fu Jing, which runs adjacent to the Beijing Hotel in a north-south direction. It is easy to locate: on leaving the Beijing Hotel simply take the first turn to the left.

Fragrant Hills (Xiang Shan)

The Fragrant Hill area is one of the most delightful spots outside Beijing and a visit there makes a pleasant excursion. It is located in the northwest of Beijing, past the Summer Palace, and can be reached comfortably in an hour by car. There is an excellent restaurant in the park, open every day, where you may eat à la carte without prior reservation. However, if you wish to make absolutely sure of a table, ask your guide or the hotel desk to call the restaurant at 819244. You can order a banquet if you wish or simply make a table reservation.

When you are traveling to the Fragrant Hills, you will pass by some interesting sites, some of which are accessible to visitors. Leaving Beijing, you take the road to the Summer Palace, follow the east wall to the Jade Fountain with its two pagodas (closed to visitors), then continue northwest. Soon after you will note the red and yellow roof of Ming Emperor Jing Tai's stele tower on the north side of the road. Keep going northwest until you come to the crossroads. Turn right and follow the road leading north. The south road leads to Badachu, or the Eight Great Sites, where there are eight old temples, all closed. Soon you will come to the Temple of the Reclining Buddha.

The **Wofosi**, as it is called in Chinese, stands behind a three-arched portico; you reach it by following the stone path lined on either side by ancient cypress trees. The temple was founded under the Tang, but was enlarged and rebuilt several times during the centuries that followed. There used to be two reclining buddhas in the temple. Now little is left, as the original statues were smashed during the Cultural Revolution and replaced by one of Mao Zedong. Mao's statue has since been removed, leaving only one bronze statue of the Buddha to see. This is probably a later copy of the original cast in 1331, but is still centuries old.

Return to the main road and proceed in the same direction, then turn right toward the hills. Soon you will come to a village; at the end of the village square take the right fork and follow it until you reach the Temple of Azure Clouds, or Biyunsi.

The **Biyunsi** was built in the fourteenth century (1366), later fell into decline, and was thereafter restored under the Ming. The Qing Emperor, Qian Long, had the diamond throne pagoda built in 1792; this edifice—consisting of a terrace, a tall pagoda at the center, and six stupas around the perimeter—is still standing. However, of the pavilions only two now house statues of the Buddha: the Hall of the Maitreya (Coming) Buddha, featuring a fine seated statue, and the Hall of the Five Hundred Luohan (to the left after passing through the Hall of the Five Pusas). Sun Yatsen's body lay in the Baiyunsi after he died, but was transferred to the mausoleum in Nanjing in 1929.

To reach the park of the Fragrant Hills, return to the village square and take the road leading up the hill to the right. The park, known as Xiang Shan Park, has a long history. The area was frequently used by the emperors of succeeding dynasties, many of whom used to hunt there. Emperor Qian Long (1736–1796) of the Qing had it developed into one of the most beautiful parks in China. Many pavilions were built, pagodas and temples erected, a wall constructed around the park, and game reintroduced. During the nineteenth and twentieth centuries the park fell into disuse, and it was considerably damaged in 1860 by the Anglo-French forces and again in 1900 during the Boxer Rebellion. Some restoration work has been undertaken in the last few decades, and the park and its buildings are in much better condition.

You may care to wander along the paths amid the pine forests and, if you are really energetic, climb to the top of the mountain at the back by following the path along the northern (upper) wall. Only the fit should undertake this climb; the path is broken and gets steep towards the top. You may prefer to seek out the old buildings. If so, you will want to visit the Luminous Temple, or Zhao Miao, the former Panchen Lama's residence, built in 1780. It is easily recognized by its "Tibetan" style and the five porticoes standing before it.

Slightly above and to the west of the temple is a seven-story pagoda faced with glazed tiles with bronze bells hanging from the corner of each roof. You can get a good view into the Luminous Temple from the pagoda.

Close by but further to the north is the Pavilion of Introspection, which is not of great architectural interest.

In the southeast corner of the park you will find the remains of the Xiang Shan Temple. Only the terraces are left, but they will convey an idea of the immense size of this temple.

Christian Churches

Although Christianity came to China for the first time through Nestorian Christian priests as early as the ninth century, it did not really take root until the thirteenth century under the Yuan. The Franciscan and Jesuit missions from Rome were the first to establish themselves with any degree of permanence in Beijing. Over the centuries that followed, the Christian religion was subject to widely differing attitudes by the reigning sovereign. During some periods it was encouraged, during others treated with suspicion, and from time to time it was driven out.

The Eastern Church, or Dong Tang, located in Wang Fu Jing, was built on the site of the house occupied by the well-known Jesuit Father Adam Schall. After he died in 1666 part of the house was converted into a small church, and after the Jesuits were suppressed the Lazarists of Portugal used it. They were expelled under the reign of Jia Qing (1796–1821), but the site was returned to them after the Anglo-French military conquest in 1860. The second Dong Tang was then built but was in turn destroyed during the Boxer Rebellion in 1900.

The present building, which can only be viewed from the street, is in a state of dilapidation and is not used. The gateway to the grounds is closed and it is not possible to enter.

The next longest-established church still in existence is the Bei Tang, or Northern Cathedral, located a few blocks west of Bei Hai. The edifice is still standing but the two spires are gone. It is now being used as a school. You can get a good glimpse of this old church through the gateway leading into the grounds. This is the third Bei Tang; it was consecrated in 1889 and restored after the Boxer Rebellion in 1900. The first Bei Tang was built at the end of the seventeenth century but destroyed in 1827. The second was built on the ruins of the first after 1860 and destroyed in 1911. The third is located on a different site from the first two, having been moved by imperial edict that it cast an "unlucky shadow" over the palaces in the Zhongnanhai.

The Southern Cathedral, or Nan Tang, erected in 1703, was built on the site of the house where the well-known missionary Matteo Ricci lived. The building standing today is the fourth Nan Tang, the other three having been destroyed during the various rebellions that took place over the two and a half centuries that followed its consecration.

The Catholic Bishop of Beijing, Michael Fu Tieshan, who was ordained in 1979, celebrates mass at the Nan Tang. This church has become the main place of worship for Catholics in Beijing. The mass is said in Latin, a rarity in the world. On special religious occasions such as Christmas and Easter an exceptionally good Chinese choir sings the choral portion of the mass. Religious services are attended by Chinese, as well as foreigners, following the relaxation of controls by the authorities after the Cultural Revolution ended. The Southern Cathedral is located in Xuan Wu Men Street a few blocks south of West Chang An Jie.

The Mishitang or Rice Market Church, located just one block north of Chang'an Boulevard in Dongdan Street, is now considered the center of the Protestant faith in China. The church was built in 1915 and takes its name from a rice market that was once located on the site.

The other church used for Protestant services is located off Chong Wenmen Street on the north side of Chang An Jie. It too is used by the foreign residents in Beijing and practicing Chinese Protestants, the numbers of whom have increased considerably since freedom of religious belief has been permitted by the authorities.

Museums

Beijing has a number of fine museums. With your program so full it will be difficult to visit more than one or perhaps two at most.

One of the richest collections of objects is housed in the *Museum of the Forbidden City.* You will visit the museum on your tour of the "inner palaces"; the Hall of the Preservation of Harmony (or Bao He Dian) has a permanent exhibition of works of art and archeological finds. Many of the outer palaces of the Forbidden City have been converted into museums, some with permanent exhibitions. If you have a particular interest in the imperial art treasures you should ask your guide for advice on which palace-museums to visit and which exhibitions are currently open. You could spend days, if not weeks, going through the museums of Beijing.

The *Museum of Chinese History,* located in the right wing of the large building flanking the eastern side of Tian An Men Square, has a fine collection of exhibits with a great appeal to visitors. The museum covers Chinese history from its origins up to the end of the Opium War of the mid-nineteenth century. The periods of history are divided into three; primitive society, covering the Paleolithic era down to B.C. 4,000; slave society, B.C. 2100–475; and feudal society, which in the eyes of the Chinese lasted from B.C. 475 through to the mid-twentieth century. You should be aware that many of the exhibits are copies of originals or restorations made from historic drawings or plans. Nevertheless, there are a great many valuable objects on display and the collection as a whole conveys a good impression of the evolution of history over a period spanning half a million years.

One of the most exciting exhibits features the life-size clay soldiers and horses excavated from the tomb of the first Qin emperor.

The *Museum of the Revolution* occupies the left wing of the building flanking the eastern side of Tian An Men and is adjacent to the Museum of History. This museum covers a period from 1840 to the 1960's. There are three major sections: the first covers the revolutionary period between 1840–1911; the second covers revolutionary events between 1911–1949; and the third covers the revolutionary period 1949 to the 1960's. The museum was closed following the Cultural Revolution of 1966 but has since re-opened.

If you are interested in what is happening in the visual and graphic arts under the Communists, you might care to visit the *National Art*

Gallery located in Chaoyang Men Street. It is located almost due north of the Peking Hotel and can be reached from there by walking along the Wang Fu Jing in a northerly direction for about ten minutes until you reach the major crossroads. It stands on the northwestern corner, and its "Sino-Soviet modern" style of architecture is unmistakable. Normally, you must obtain prior permission for a visit.

Some visitors are interested in the culture of the national minorities who reside in China and may wish to visit the *Minorities Cultural Palace Museum* located at the western end of Chang An Boulevard. Apart from an interesting exhibition featuring certain aspects of the minority cultures, this institute also houses the students from the national minorities who are undergoing training as cadres to carry the revolutionary ideology back to their respective cultural groups.

The *Lu Xun Museum* will interest visitors who are students of modern Chinese literature. It is devoted, of course, to the most admired revolutionary writer in China, Lu Xun (1881–1936). The museum was built to the east of the house Lu Xun lived in for a time.

Sun Yatsen Park

Beijing has some fine parks to explore, these often providing a welcome relief from the hectic pace of a busy tour program. Although some are located on the outskirts of Beijing, there are many quite near the central hotels. The main entrance to Sun Yatsen Park, or Zhong Shan Gong Yuan, is through a gateway about a hundred yards or so west of Tian An Men gate. There is also another entrance on the left of the Meridian Gate to the Forbidden City.

When you enter the main gate you will pass under a white marble *pai lou* which has three passageways. Follow the path as it turns left and take the first turn to your right towards the gateway in the wall. Note the beautiful cypress trees, many of which are thought to be over a thousand years old; note also the small pavilion with the single glazed tile roof in orange.

After you pass through the gateway you will see a fan-shaped modern theater with large columns to your right, built in a design completely out of character with the rest of the buildings in the park. Ahead of you is the Altar of the Earth and Harvests. The Altar is surrounded by a small square wall faced with orange tiles to the south, blue tiles to the east, black to the north, and yellow to the west. The passageway through each wall passes under a *pai lou.* Inside the walls there are three tiers, square-shaped, leading to the top surface which is the altar. Step up the three tiers and you will see that the top surface is hard-packed earth divided into four areas, represented by earth of different colors: red to the south, yellow in the middle, black to the north, white to the west, and green to the east. This earth was originally carried to the Altar from the four corners of the empire and symbolized the principle that the "Son of Heaven" owned everything on earth.

The emperor came here twice a year to make sacrifices to the gods so that sowing would be successful and the crop bountiful. North of the altar stand two pavilions; the first is the Hall of Prayer, the second the Hall of Halberds.

There are numerous other interesting corners of this park, the most popular area lying in the southwest and featuring attractively decorated covered walks. There is also a hothouse which provides welcome warmth in the freezing winter months.

People's Cultural Park

Known as Renmin Wen Hua Gong to the Chinese, the site of this park is the "twin" of the Sun Yatsen Park, lying on the eastern side of the Tian An Men Gate. Again, the main access is through a gateway in the wall a few hundred yards or so east of Tian An Men or by a gateway to the right of the Meridian Gate to the Forbidden City.

Inside the entrance there are magnificent cypress trees surrounding a large paved area. Cross the courtyard towards the gate with three enormous studded doorways. Pass through the gate and cross one of the bridges spanning the small stream. The steps then lead through the Da Ji Men Gate to another courtyard. Beyond, a large pavilion known as the Qian Dian stands on a three-tiered terrace. It has the traditional twin roofs of orange tiles. The gargoyles at the corners of the building are particularly well carved. The central marble ramp of the stairways to the top of the terrace has a design-motif of horses, lions, and dragons. Inside there are ten huge central columns of timber supporting a roof which has a fine coffered ceiling. The building was used for ceremonies associated with the Tablets of the Ancestors.

The Zhong Dian, or Middle Hall, which is to the north of the first building, was used to store the tablets when they were not being used in the ceremonies. A third hall stands on a separate terrace north of the Middle Hall.

Other Parks

If you are a park-lover you will want to continue your explorations, and you should next try to see the Temple of the Sun Park, or Ritan Gong Yuan, located only a few hundred yards from the International Club. Although it has not yet been fully restored, there are some interesting old pavilions, one of which has been converted into a restaurant (closed Fridays) where perhaps the best *jiaozi* in Beijing are served. You can also visit the site of what was once an Altar to the Sun. This site is surrounded by a circular wall, but inside nothing is left of the original altar.

Another park worth visiting is the Zi Zhu Yuan, or Purple Bamboo Park, adjacent to the zoo in the northwestern sector of Beijing. It has fine walks, a lovely lake, and attractive scenery.

Another park worth visiting is Joyous Pavilion Park, or Tao Ran Ting, located slightly west of the southern end of Qian Men Street and not far from the Temple of Heaven. It also features a lake and has a number of pavilions where you may sit and relax.

Other Places of Interest

For those who are inexhaustible or have special interests, there is even more to see and do. For example, you may care to take a ride on the *Beijing Subway*. You cannot just go there and buy a ticket, however, but must make arrangements through your guide.

Work on the subway commenced in 1965 and the first line was completed in October 1969. The subway has seventeen stations along fifteen miles of track. It carries 70–80,000 passengers daily at a cost of ¥0.10 per ride. The trains travel at an average of 35 miles per hour. The subway is open between 6 A.M. and 9 P.M. You will be impressed by its cleanliness.

Another attraction is the *Beijing Zoo*, located in the northwest sector of the city not far from the Exhibition Center. It has an interesting display of animals, but undoubtedly the most popular are the pandas, which are to be found not far from the entrance. If you would rather eat and watch the animals than watch the animals eating, you can do so at the Russian Restaurant, which has large windows overlooking the zoo.

For those interested in astronomy, a trip to the Beijing Planetarium will prove interesting. It is located in San Lihe Road only a short distance from the Beijing Zoo and the Capital Gymnasium.

Another favorite is the Old Observatory. You will see it on the right-hand side of the road when you are traveling along Chang An Jie toward the International Club. It is a rather stark, fortlike building with an array of astronomical instruments on the balcony. Kubilai Khan's observatory was built on the site, but the building you see today is relatively modern and of little architectural interest. However, the instruments on the balcony attract the attention of visitors (sextant, quadrant, and celestial globe).

There are interesting historical references to the Observatory. First constructed in 1296, under Kubilai Khan, it then marked the southeast corner of the city walls protecting the capital. It was built because Kubilai wanted to draw up a new calendar, the one that existed then being inaccurate. Centuries later, the astronomers of the day were replaced by Jesuit missionaries from Europe, who were more advanced in the science of heavenly bodies. In 1674, the ruling Qing emperor had Father Verbiest build a set of five astronomical instruments to complement the one sent as a gift to the emperor by Louis XIV. These were removed by the Germans after the Allied Powers intervention in 1900 during the Boxer Rebellion. They were returned in 1919 and are presumably the instruments now standing on the Observatory terrace.

If you like old bridges you will want to see the Marco Polo Bridge, which spans the river Yong Ding southwest of Beijing. The bridge has been given its name because it was described by Marco Polo when he visited China in the thirteenth century. He thought it was one of the most beautiful bridges he had ever seen. It was first constructed in 1192 and restored in the fifteenth century and again at the end of the seventeenth. It is 770 feet long and has 11 arches and many stone columns along the parapets at either side. There are two stone elephants at either end. In Chinese, the bridge is called Luoguoqiao. It holds a place in modern history for what became known as the "Marco Polo Bridge Incident" in 1937, which led to full-scale resistance against the Japanese in the Sino-Japanese War.

Many visitors are interested in the old Foreign Legation Area, which is located only a few hundred yards from the Xin Qiao Hotel. Not much remains of the old embassies now and it looks as though the whole area is due for demolition soon. An easy landmark is St. Michaels Church with its twin gothic towers and dangling cross. Opposite it is the old French Embassy. As you stroll along "Legation Street," now known as Dong Jiao Min Xiang, you will pass a number of buildings that were former embassies, all of them in poor condition. It is doubtful whether your guide will be able to identify many of them.

Visitors who are members of the teaching profession may be interested in touring Beijing University (known as "Bei Da"), the Qinghua University, or the Beijing Languages Institute. You can go to these establishments by making arrangements through your guide. If you or a member of your group wishes to make a visit, you should raise the subject with your guide as early as possible. The same applies to tourists who wish to visit the Beijing Library.

Requests to visit jails or courts are now occasionally granted so there is no harm in asking.

If you are a Moslem and wish to attend an Islamic religious service, you can visit the Beijing Mosque used by Beijing's foreign resident community. It is located in the southwest sector of Beijing. Your guide will make the necessary arrangements.

Visitors with an interest in archeology may wish to make an excursion to the prehistoric site at Zhou Kou Dian where bones of "Beijing Man" were excavated in 1929. The excavation was most important in the development of theories relating to the origin of man. Studies have shown that the fragments of human bone are about 500,000 years old. The site is located about 30 miles southwest of Beijing and is of very little interest to the general tourist. Special permission must be obtained to visit the area, which is outside the jurisdiction of the Beijing security apparatus.

PRACTICAL INFORMATION FOR BEIJING

 FACTS AND FIGURES. Beijing lies at about the same latitude as Philadelphia, Indianapolis, and Denver. It is about 1,400 miles by air from Tokyo, about 4 hours actual flying time on the fastest direct service. Time difference is one hour. Other distances: 698 miles northwest of Shanghai by air, 2 hours' direct flight; 915 miles northwest of Shanghai by rail, 26 hours' train journey; 1,150 miles north of Canton by air, 34–35 hours' train journey.

Beijing is 165 feet above sea level.

The following table shows the average temperature per month along with the monthly high-low readings in °F.

PEKING TEMPERATURE RANGE (°F)

Month	High	Average	Low
January	50	22	−9
February	58	27	−2
March	71	38	7
April	87	55	26
May	94	66	38
June	101	74	51
July	103	77	60
August	100	75	53
September	89	66	·39
October	83	53	27
November	73	38	0
December	55	26	−3

WHEN TO GO. The best times of the year to visit Beijing are late spring or early summer (May to mid-June) and autumn (late August to early November).

Winter is dry and cold with short days and infrequent light snowfalls. There are biting winds which deposit a fine yellow silt-dust from the northern plateau and desert regions onto the city. The relative humidity drops considerably and you will receive a zap of static electricity every time you touch a metal object. Even kisses between the fleshiest of lips are subject to these electrostatic forces unless the participants are cautious enough to ground themselves beforehand. Thus for many reasons a winter visit to Beijing is not recommended. Of course, a winter visit is better than no visit at all.

Spring arrives in April, but after a week or so of warmer weather which brings out tiny green leaf-buds on the trees, dust storms sweep out of Central Asia and deposit more. Fortunately these unpleasant winds usually stop by mid-May. You will also note that the average temperature rises from about 38°F. to 55°F. from March to April and from 55°F. to 66°F. from April to May.

Summer begins at the end of May or early June and, as the season progresses, temperatures and humidity build up, reaching a peak in July and August. Coinciding with the spells of oppressive heat when temperatures occasionally exceed 100°F. there are periods of heavy rainfall. Insignificant until June, most of Beijing's 25-inch per annum rainfall is concentrated in June and July, and there are often sudden thunderstorms, usually in the late afternoon.

Autumn is a delightful period in Beijing, by far the best season of all, and usually extends from early September through mid-November. The days are pleasantly warm, the humidity at optimum levels, and the evenings possess a faint refreshing coolness. The forest of trees growing in the city gradually turn to gold until, in mid-November, the temperatures begin to drop suddenly, the winter winds begin to reassert their authority, and the leaves are torn violently from the trees.

HOW TO GET THERE. There are direct flights to Beijing from many cities around the world. The nearest international airport is Hong Kong, 2 hours 40 minutes away by jet.

The other way to enter China is by rail, from Hong Kong or via the USSR. The journey from Hong Kong to Beijing, though a long one, is an interesting experience. If takes about 36 hours, with two nights on the train. You are accommodated in sleeping compartments for up to four people. It is preferable to avoid long train journeys in summer; many of the trains operating in China lack air-conditioning. Check with your guide or at your hotel.

Another alternative is to travel from Hong Kong to Guangzhou (Canton) by boat, hovercraft, or bus, and then take a domestic flight to Beijing.

LOCAL TIME. Beijing standard time applies throughout the whole of China. When it is midday in Beijing it is 9 P.M. the previous day in San Francisco and midnight the previous day in New York.

HOW TO GET AROUND. Normally your travel arrangements in Beijing will be handled by your guide. If you are in a group you may be assigned a minibus or coach, depending on the size of the group. Otherwise you will be provided with a car and driver.

Bicycle: Undoubtedly the best way of getting around is by bicycle. When the weather is good there is no better way of seeing the city. You can cycle down the narrow *hutungs* (lanes), peek into the Chinese courtyards, and see the Beijing that most visitors miss. You will need the map in this guidebook to help you find your way. Alternatively, a map of Beijing in English is available at the bookstalls of major hotels, but it will not show the location of all the sites you may wish to visit.

You can hire one for a small fee at the Jianguomenwai Bicycle Repair Shop (6 A.M.–6 P.M.; Tel. 59.23.91) located opposite the Friendship Store. However, you can do so only after handing over a letter of introduction from either the China International Travel Service or your Embassy, or by leaving your passport as security.

On Foot The next best way to see the nearby streets of Beijing is on foot. You can wander at will in the vicinity of your hotel, or take a bus and then stroll around. Again, you can use the map in this guidebook, but you should obtain a map of bus routes from your hotel if you are going to travel further afield.

Taxi Another alternative is to hire a taxi through the lobby desk of your hotel. Two car sizes are available: one holding four passengers, the other holding three. The larger size taxi is slightly more expensive. It is seldom possible to hail a passing taxi; they are not distinguished by colors or signs, and if you did manage to stop one you would have to communicate with the driver. In general, then, taxis must be arranged by telephone. The line for English-speaking dispatchers of the major fleet, Shoudou (Capital) Taxi Company is 55.74.61. Ask how long you can expect to wait before your taxi will arrive. A wait of 15–30 minutes is not unusual.

If you are going shopping or attending a business appointment, have your taxi wait for you. Waiting time is inexpensive and you will save yourself the inconvenience of getting another and avoid a long wait. If you get stuck somewhere without transport you should either telephone a taxi company or call your hotel and ask them to send a taxi.

Taxis have no meters. The fare is calculated by reference to the odometer and based on the number of kilometers' run plus waiting time. You will be given ticketlike receipts with western numerals on them. The drivers are completely honest, even though the same trip may cost slightly different fares. Try to carry small notes; the drivers are usually short of change. Do not tip the driver.

Car Rental: You can arrange to hire a car and driver the entire day through CITS by calling 55.41.92. Chauffer-driven cars can also be rented through National Car Rental at rates ranging from US$14 to $20 daily, US$100 to $150

BEIJING

weekly. You can even hire the famous Red Flag limousine with chauffeur for about US$30 per day. Bookings for all cars can be made prior to your departure through National's reservation system by calling (in U.S.A.) 800: 227–7368 or when in Beijing, 556531 X7087.

Bus Rental. National also hire buses and mini-buses with drivers. In the U.S. arrangements can be made by calling 800: 227–7268. In Beijing chauffeured buses or mini-buses can be hired by calling 86.36.61.

Tour Buses. You can take inexpensive tour buses to a number of outlying sites in Beijing from Qianmen bus station (2 Qianmen Dong Av.) Call Tourist Motor Corp. of Beijing; Tel. 75.54.14 or 75.52.46. Information about departure times and tickets can be obtained from the company, your guide, or your hotel.

Public Transport. If you can speak some Chinese or are adventurous, you may care to get out on your own and use the public transport system in Beijing: the buses, trolley cars, and subway. Fares are very cheap, but be warned—public transport is jammed during peak hours and crowded most of the time. The subway is clean and quiet with plenty of seats available in off–peak periods.

MONEY. You can change money conveniently at the cashier's desk in your hotel lobby or at the bank within the building of the Friendship Store. However, in case you need to visit the head office of the Bank of China at 17 Xijiaominxiang, the business hours are as follows:

Summer: Mon.-Fri., 9:30 A.M.-12 noon, 2 P.M.-5 P.M. Sat., 9:30 A.M.-12 noon. Sun., closed.

Winter: Mon.-Fri., 9:30 A.M.-12 noon, 1:40 P.M.-4:30 P.M. Sat., 9:30 A.M.-12 noon. Sun., closed.

You may telephone the Bank and usually find someone who speaks English: 338521, 330452, or 330887.

All notes and coins have Western numerals, so you will find them easy to identify. The largest note is Yuan 10, written ¥10; other notes circulated are ¥5, ¥2, and ¥1. Smaller notes are also used: ¥0.50, ¥0.20, ¥0.10. The Yuan is composed of 100 fen. 10 fen equal 1 Jiao (known as "Mao"). There are 5-fen, 2-fen, and 1-fen coins. Dividing the Chinese figure by 1.8 will give you the rough equivalent in American dollars.

MEDICAL SERVICES. The only hospital that caters to foreigners is the Capital Hospital (tel. 553731 extn. 565, 274, or 276), located at North Dongan St., one block north of Chang'an Boulevard.

The outpatient clinic is open each morning from 8 A.M. to 11:30 A.M. from Monday to Saturday. It is also open from 2 P.M. to 4:30 P.M. on Mondays, Thursdays, and Fridays. On passing through the entrance gates, go up the stairs to the right and enter the building immediately ahead of you. English is spoken.

Emergency cases are, of course, accepted at any time. There is no ambulance service available, unless you wish to follow the practice of the locals and have yourself pedaled to hospital lying on the back of a three-wheeled cart. But the hotel staff will be more than sympathetic to your distress and arrange a car to take you to the hospital without any delay.

Many of the hospital staff speak English, but an interpreter may be useful. You will normally be charged for medicines, drugs, and materials used. Consultation fees are very low—usually a few yuan.

The Vaccination Center (tel. 461857) is located at Ho Ping Li North Street.

CHURCH SERVICES. There are two Christian churches holding services on Sunday mornings and a Moslem mosque holding services every Friday. The Protestant Church is situated in Dong Dan near the Capital Hospital, and the Roman Catholic Church (Nan Tang) at Xuan Wu Men in the southwest of the city (see map). Inquiries about times of services, which appear to vary from time to time, should be made to your hotel, guide, or embassy.

If you are travelling in a group tour, you will normally find your tour program fairly full, even on Sunday, so if you wish to break from your group to attend a service, let your guide know.

WHAT TO SEE. You could spend weeks exploring Beijing and still not see everything. The old Forbidden City, home of the Ming and Qing emperors, would take days to explore thoroughly. Then there are excursions to the Ming Tombs and the Great Wall, explorations of the Summer Palace, and visits to the Temple of Heaven, Bei Hai, Coal Hill, and a host of other places.

You are fortunate if you have a few weeks to spend in Beijing or can return regularly to seek out its treasures. Most visitors have only a week at the most, and sometimes less, to explore the city and its surroundings, and face problems arranging a program to include all the places of interest. To help you get the most out of your visit, these places have been grouped under "major sites," which really should not be missed: a "selection" of temples, towers, and pagodas; places which best convey the "atmosphere" of present-day Beijing; parks and museums; and finally a miscellaneous group for visitors with special interests or sufficient time to explore in full.

A five-day tour program for Beijing has been drawn up which will allow you to take in the most important places of interest over the first three days. These are places that all visitors usually want to see. The remaining two days have been set aside to allow you to make a choice, according to your particular interests, from the various categories. For instance, you may prefer to spend the last two days antique-hunting and visiting the sites of the old Christian churches. Or you may wish to visit Beijing's parks and museums. The program allows you to see the most important places and, at the same time, pursue your particular interests.

FIVE-DAY PROGRAM

Day 1: Morning: Tian An Men Square; there you will see the Tian An Men Gate, the Great Hall of the People, the Mausoleum of Mao Zedong, the Qian Men Gate. Temple of Heaven.

Lunch: Hotel.

Afternoon: The Forbidden City.

Day 2: Full Day: The Great Wall of China. Ming Tombs.

The Great Wall and the Ming Tombs are convenient to visit in one day if you are going by car. If you are going by train you will not be able to visit the Ming Tombs en route and should arrange to visit the site by car on another (half) day.

Day 3: Morning: Summer Palace Lake.

Lunch: "Ting Li Guan" Restaurant at the Summer Palace.

Afternoon: Bei Hai Park.

Jingshan (Coal Hill) Park, or shopping.

You are advised to make a luncheon reservation at the "Ting Li Guan" before departure, preferably the day before. You may order a banquet or simply reserve a number of places and eat à la carte. Have your guide or hotel clerk telephone 281936. See "Restaurants Outside Beijing" in the "Dining Out" section.

Days 4 and 5: Program to be drawn up according to your own particular interests. Consult the following lists.

Don't forget that you will probably have an hour or two to spare on some days, *e.g.,* on Day 2 you will normally get back to your hotel at 4 P.M. If you are tired you can take a short nap, then slip down to the Friendship Store (open every day; closes 7 P.M. in summer and 6:30 P.M. in winter) or elsewhere to begin your bargain hunting.

Places of Major Interest
Tian An Men Square and Surroundings
Imperial Palaces of the Old Forbidden City
Temple of Heaven
Great Wall
Ming Tombs
Summer Palace
Bei Hai Lake and Park
Jingshan (or Coal Hill) Park

Selected Temples and Pagodas
Lama Temple
Temple of the White Dagoba (similar to the one in Bei Hai Park)
Great Bell Temple
Drum Tower
Bell Tower
Temple of the Five Pagodas
Yellow Temple
Former Temple of Confucius
Former Imperial College

Beijing Atmosphere

(Note: Visits to these places can be combined with shopping expeditions. But you should wander into the side streets to get the "feel" of life in Beijing.)

Qian Men Street
Wang Fu Jing
Liu Li Chang
Zhongwenmen
Dongdan Covered Market

Fragrant Hills

A delightful place to "get away from it all" where there are pleasant walks amid the pines, where the remains of old temples are to be found, and where the energetic can scale the nearby mountain peaks. You may also have lunch at the Fragrant Hills Restaurant; reservations are usually not necessary, but if you wish to be on the safe side have your guide call 819244 before you set out. You can eat à la carte if you do not wish to order a banquet.

Parks
Bei Hai Park
Jingshan (or Coal Hill) Park
Sun Yatsen Park
People's Cultural Park
Temple of the Sun Park
Purple Bamboo Park
Joyous Pavilion Park

Old Christian Churches

(Note: All except the Nan Tang (Catholic Church) and the main Protestant Church off Dongsi St. are used for non-religious purposes and can only be viewed from the outside.)

Dong Tang or Eastern Church
Bei Tang or Former Northern Church
Nan Tang or Southern Cathedral (Catholic)
St. Michael's
Protestant Church of Peking (Mishitang)

Museums
Imperial Palace Museum
Museum of Chinese History
Museum of the Chinese Revolution
National Art Museum
Minorities Cultural Palace Museum
Lu Xun Museum

Other Places of Interest
Beijing Subway
Beijing Zoo
Planetarium
Old Observatory
Marco Polo Bridge
Former Legation Area
Beijing University
Qin Hua University
Beijing Languages Institute
Beijing Library
Beijing Mosque
Zhou Kou Dian ("Peking Man")
Natural Science Museum
Old Summer Palace

SPORTS. Recreational facilities are available only at the International Club (tel. 522144; closed Mondays). There is no entrance fee or regular subscription required, and the club is open to all foreigners. An enormous *swimming pool* is open during the summer months. To use it you must obtain a swimming license from the pool attendant, who will need a passport-size photograph to seal onto the license. You must first visit the Capital Hospital (Tuesday and Thursday afternoons from 3 P.M. onwards, but get there at 2:30 P.M. to avoid long lines) for a medical—mainly to test your blood pressure, ears, eyes, nose, and throat. You normally need to bring a passport photo there, too. Obviously, all this rigmarole would not suit the busy tourist, but a businessman who is often in for protracted spells of doing nothing between appointments will find the effort worthwhile.

Tennis players will be pleased to note that there are five outdoor tennis courts. The courts are open from 9 A.M. to noon and from 3 P.M. to 7 P.M. Racquets and balls cannot be rented at the Club, so you must bring your own or purchase them in Beijing. Local racquets are relatively cheap, but balls are expensive. Neither is of a quality that meets approved international tournament standards, but they are quite suitable for the average player.

There are two indoor tennis courts open all year round; charges are higher when the overhead lights are used. The courts, dusty and bumpy as they are, provide welcome exercise in winter and are open daily (except Mondays) from 9 A.M. until 9 P.M., with no break during lunch hours.

If you do not have a partner you can hire the services of one of the Chinese court attendants, who are all good players. You will be able to play a match against them or just hit-up.

There are also *badminton* facilities available; to make arrangements you should call the Club in advance. Equipment cannot be rented from the Club but can be purchased locally at low-cost.

There are seven *billiard* tables—five large and two small. Generally speaking, the cues and balls at this club and the other places in Beijing (*e.g.*, larger hotels catering to foreigners) are in pretty bad shape. Unless you are a serious player you will find that these imperfect instruments lend a certain hilarity to the game.

There are five *table tennis* tables and the Club will provide bats and balls.

A marker service is available for both billiards and table tennis. Your idle youth may have endowed you with sufficient prowess on the green baize for you to annihilate your marker, but you will be lucky indeed to possess the footwork and agility necessary to defeat a Chinese table tennis player.

There are two indoor *bowling alleys* of a sort that only exist now in Museums of Sport. But they provide a lot of fun. The two lanes are not automatic and players must fix their own pins.

SHOPPING. You will best savor the atmosphere of Beijing by taking a walk in any of the main shopping areas. You will then become part of the bustling crowds of Chinese on the streets and in the shops, and will see the variety of goods available—all produced locally (except for the high-priced Swiss watches) and all on sale (as distinct from many of the goods in Soviet shop windows).

When you go to a counter, the locals will pull back to let you be served first, and watch with curiosity as you buy. Give them a smile and you'll get one back. A small crowd may gather, but it's all part of the fun. Curious children will probably follow you around for a while. Smile and say "Hello" in Chinese, *Nin hao,* and they will usually draw back shyly and melt into the crowd.

There are a number of large shopping areas in central Beijing that you will find interesting. They are:

Wangfujing, old "Morrison Street"; go on foot.

Dongdan and Chong Wen Men Dajie, parallel to Wang Fu Jing and one block east of the Peking Hotel; go on foot unless you are in a hurry.

Qian Men, directly south of the Qian Men Gate; short taxi ride.

Xi Dan, go west along Chang An from the Beijing Hotel and turn right just after the PTT Building; take a taxi.

Liu Li Chang, southwest of Qian Men; take a taxi.

Friendship Store. The easiest way to shop is to visit the Friendship Store, but it does not convey a Chinese atmosphere, being there to serve foreigners only.

It is located on Chang An Jie near the International Club, and stocks a substantial range of goods: food (caviar is excellent and cheap), wine, clothing, leather coats, furs, silks, jade, jewelry, porcelain, scrolls, antiques, carpets, and giftware. There is also a tailor shop (slow); dry-cleaning service (takes a week and is expensive); and watch repair shop.

The store is open every day of the year from 9 A.M. (meat and vegetable section from 8:30 A.M.) to 6:30 P.M. in winter and 7 P.M. in summer.

There is a bank attached to the store where visitors may cash travelers' checks.

Department Stores: More interesting to visit but far more crowded and time-consuming are the two large department stores in Wang Fu Jing. One is known to foreigners as the Beijing Department Store, actually Beijing Bai Huo Da Lou, literally "Beijing Hundred Products Big Store." It has a car park area in front of it. The other is the Dong Feng (East Wind) covered market. They are opposite each other on Wang Fu Jing. Both are open from 9 A.M. to 8 P.M.

The Handicrafts Store, situated at 200 Wang Fu Jing, is worth a visit. The store is located on the right-hand side when proceeding north along Wang Fu Jing from the Beijing Hotel.

The first floor sells pottery, paper-cuts, calligraphy, and art supplies. The second floor sells linens, bamboo and cane articles, and cloisonné ware. You can also buy Chinese batik, but it is expensive compared with other Asian batik and usually not as good. You may also be asked for cotton coupons.

It is probably the best place in Beijing to buy linens; and artists will find an excellent range of good quality and inexpensive art supplies available.

A good selection of linen ware and tablecloths is also available across the street at 265 Wang Fu Jing.

The Fur Shop: Just beyond the Handicrafts Store in Wang Fu Jing, again on the eastern (right-hand) side when proceeding north, you will find the Fur Shop (192 Wang Fu Jing). It is a tiny shop and the only sign you will see is in Chinese, so keep a look out for a window with a few pelts in it. Advice on buying is given in a later section under "Furs."

The Theater Shop: Now located at 12 Chong Men Men Da Jie, not far from the Xin Qiao Hotel, the Theater Shop sells a wide range of antiques, objets d'art, and old theatrical gowns. You will find many Chinese, Japanese and European antiques, carriage clocks, monogrammed silverware, candelabra, crystal, porcelain and metalware. There are also plenty of Mongolian "hotpots," brass bedwarmers, furniture locks, wooden boxes, and metal dishes.

On the ground floor there is a section selling antique and reproduction Chinese furniture, and another selling a variety of second-hand furs, some made up into rugs and others in their natural shape.

The People's Market is really two stores connected to each other to form a large Chinese emporium. The goods on display are the same as those found in the Peking Department Store and the East Wind (Dong Feng) Market.

To go there you walk north along Wang Fu Jing from the Beijing Hotel. You will pass the Overseas Chinese Hotel and the CAAC Building on your right; continue until the first cross street. Turn right, and about 50 yards ahead to your left you will see a small lane leading northward to the entrance.

Antiques

You should always check with the vendor that the antique you are about to purchase can be taken out of China. If so, retain the invoice and make sure that the red wax seal on the item remains intact.

Probably the best place to buy antiques in Beijing is at Liu Li Chang, literally "Glazed Tile Works Street," which, about a thousand years ago, was part of the eastern section of the capital. After the Ming established the capital at Beijing, numerous tile works were established there. At the beginning of the Qing (mid-seventeenth century) small shopkeepers moved into the area, particularly booksellers, and before long the area became a meeting place for scholars. Printers and antique shops were soon established. When the area was destroyed at the end of the Qing, only the narrow winding lanes around Liu Li Chang survived. (Many shops are being renovated and have temporarily re-located to the Temple of Heaven area.)

The best and most expensive antique shops are located at 70 and 80 Liu Li Chang. They sell a range of antiques: porcelain, jade, snuff bottles, old cloisonné ware, metalware, and wood carvings.

The scroll shop at 63 Liu Li Chang sells traditional-style original paintings and old calligraphy. It is here that you can look for an original by Qi Baishi, provided you have a spare $10,000 or so.

At 136 Liu Li Chang there is a small shop selling copies of Han, Tang, and Song Dynasty ceramics. There are some beautiful pieces: small figurines, large ceramic horses, camels, pigs, and dogs—all in antique finish and excellently reproduced.

There you may also buy rubbings of bas-relief carvings from tombs, temples, and caves located at various sites in China. Some of the rubbings are from carvings that are over 2,000 years old. They make excellent gifts—they are flat, light, easy to pack, and, more to the point for the impoverished traveler, quite inexpensive. Buy a few for yourself and have them mounted when you go home. They will serve as an elegant and pleasing memento of your visit to China.

Rong Bao Zhai, or Studio of Glorious Treasures, located at 19 Liu Li Chang, (a little to the west across in Hu Fang Lu) sells watercolors, modern prints and scrolls. It trains craftsmen in wood blockprinting and reproduction of watercolor paintings. Their work is exceptionally good.

Lanterns, lamp shades, and some modern pictures may be bought at 92 Liu Li Chang.

Jade and Jewelry

There is a great variety of fine jade available in Beijing, as well as a huge range of ordinary-quality jade. Some experts say that you can purchase jade cheaper in other countries in Asia but that the risk of being deceived by fraudulent articles is quite high.

The advantage of buying in China is the feeling of security that comes from knowing that you get exactly what you pay for. Therefore, many visitors who do not understand the perplexities of the jade market are often happy to buy jade in Beijing, even though a similar article might be available outside China at a reduced price.

For the uninitiated, a visit to the Friendship Store jade counter represents the best starting point.

There is also a wonderful range of jewelry available, ranging in price from a few yuan up to thousands, in an infinite variety of styles. These items are small to pack and therefore represent sensible gift purchases for the overloaded traveler.

Chops

Chops are used in China to stamp a crest, insignia, or name on documents. They are made from a variety of stone materials ranging from onyx to jade. You can buy antique chops with someone else's name in Chinese characters or, if you wish, have your own name or insignia carved into a new set.

If you buy a pair you can have your name in Chinese characters on one and in your own language on the other. Apart from the cost of the chop itself, there is a charge per letter, depending on the size of the chop.

There are chop shops at 78 West Liu Li Chang, 35 South Xinhua Street, and at 261 Wang Fu Jing. All these shops sell the red ink traditionally used. Some residents claim that the best ink is obtained at the Beijing Department Store.

If you are uncertain about your name in Chinese, ask to consult the books there giving Chinese equivalents for names written in English and German only. Before selecting a chop you should also consult the book at the store which shows the various styles of lettering that can be engraved onto the base.

Furs

Beijing is a good place to buy furs; there is an excellent variety of pelts available, such as sable, mink, fox, and rabbit. These are all available made up into coats and hats as well as in their natural state. Mink is a good buy; the quality is not bad, and the price is certainly less than for Siberian mink. However, you will get what you pay for.

A great variety of such skins as sheep, goat, and wolf are available in natural form or made up into rugs.

Suede articles of sheepskin and pigskin are an excellent buy; the workmanship can be first-class and the price most reasonable. However, be sure to try on a number of garments to get the right fit; despite good workmanship, an occasional ill-shaped garment seems to slip through. Chinese styles tend to lag behind those of other suede centers, so you will have to be content with fairly standard styles.

When buying, use your nose. Some skins are imperfectly cured and give off a distinct odor which the buyer, concentrating on cut and color, sometimes fails to detect. On your return home you may look smart in your coat but find yourself curiously alone on the street.

Furs, pelts, skins, and a few garments are available on the second floor of the Friendship Store and at No. 192 Wang Fu Jing.

U.S. Customs prohibits the importation of furs and pelts from endangered species. Check before departing.

Carpets

Chinese carpets are world-renowned, and a fine variety is available at two locations in Beijing—on the third floor of the Friendship Store and at 208 Qian Men. Carpets, rugs, and mats are available in classical styles and in the traditional designs of the autonomous regions of China such as Xinjiang, Inner Mongolia, and Tibet. Antique finishes are available.

In general, carpets are high-priced, but the connoisseur may be able to find some bargains.

Books

Visitors who can read Chinese may wish to look in at the Xinhua Bookstore. It sells books, maps, and revolutionary posters, and is located at 214 Wang Fu Jing, close to the Peking Hotel. There is another branch inside the Dong Feng (East Wind) Market, further along Wang Fu Jing.

Foreign-language publications on Chinese affairs and international socialism are available at the Foreign Language Book Store located at 235 Wang Fu Jing. This shop also has a wide range of postcards available as well as some fine art books.

There is a second-hand foreign bookstore in the Dong Feng Market and another in the Xi Dan Market. Second-hand Chinese books may be purchased at 96 or 136 Liu Li Chang.

Stamps

Stamp collectors will be pleased to learn that the China Stamp Export Corporation located at 28 Tungan Men (off Wang Fu Jing) sells Chinese stamps minted in sets.

QUICK REFERENCE TELEPHONE GUIDE

Emergency Numbers

Capital Hospital: Clinic ("Dongmen") Dongdan Menzhenbu, tel. 55.37.31. Emergency Cases ("Ximen") 1 Shaifuyuan Hutong, tel. 55.37.31, or x251,x217,x276.

Fire Brigade: tel. 09.

Frequently Used Numbers

International Telephone Calls: 33.74.31 (for information call 116).

Long distance calls within China, English speaking: 55.35.36

Long distance calls within China; Chinese-speaking: 113 (for information on local calls dial 114)

Taxis: Shoudou (Capital) Taxi Company tel. 557461.

International Club, Jianguomenwai, tel. 522144.

Friendship Store, Jianguomenwai, tel. 593531.

Bank of China, Xijiaominxiang 17, tel. 338521.

Post Office, 23 Dong Dan Bei Dajie, tel. 555414.

PTT Building (for information about cables and telex) tel. 664900.

Public Security Bureau *(Foreigners Section),* Nan Chi Zi, tel. 553102.

Vaccination Center, He Ping Li Bei Jie, tel. 461857.

Embassy Telephone Numbers

Diplomatic Service Bureau: Enquiries: 557049

Europe
Austria: 522061
Belgium: 521736
Bulgaria: 522232
Czechoslovakia: 521530
Denmark: 522431

Finland: 521753
France: 521331
East Germany: 521631
West Germany: 522161
Greece: 521391
Hungary: 521431

Italy: 522131
Netherlands: 521731
Norway: 522261
Poland: 521235
Rumania: 523255
Spain: 521967
Sweden: 521770
Switzerland: 522831
USSR: 522051
United Kingdom: 521961
Yugoslavia: 521562

Australasia
Australia: 522331
New Zealand: 522731

The Americas
Argentina: 522090
Brazil: 522740
Canada: 521475
Chile: 521522
Cuba: 521714
Guyana: 521337
Mexico: 522070
Peru: 522178
USA: 522033–39
Venezuela: 521295

USEFUL ADDRESSES AND TELEPHONE NUMBERS

Airlines

Civil Aviation Administration of China (CAAC): city office Dongsixi St. 117. Tel. 558861.

information. Dongsixi St. 117. Tel. 554415.
information Beijing Airport. Tel. 552515 (or switchboard: 55.83.41).
cargo: international Dongsixi St. Tel. 552945.
Aeroflot, Jianguomenwai 2-2-41. Tel. 523203.
Air France, Jianguomenwai 2-2-21. Tel. 523894.
Air Romania, Rumanian Embassy. Tel. 523552.
Ethiopian Air, Jianguomenwai 2-2-22. Tel. 523285.
Iran Air, Jianguomenwai 2-2-51. Tel. 523249 or 523843.
Japan Air Lines, Jianguomenwai 2-2-12. Tel. 523457 or 523374.
Pakistan Airlines, Jianguomenwai 2-2-61. Tel. 523542 or 523989.
Philippine Airlines, Jianguomenwai 2-2-11. Tel. 523992.
Swiss Air, Jianguomenwai 2-2-81. Tel. 523284.
Yugoslav Airlines, Jianguomenwai 2-2-162. Tel. 523486.

Travel

China International Travel Service (CITS), 6 Dong Chang An Ave. (opp. Beijing Hotel):
Switchboard, tel. 551031; American and Oceanic Division, tel. 557558; Japanese Division, tel. 551826; First European Division, tel. 553121; Second European Division, tel. 555078; Asian, African, Latin American Division, tel. 557908; China Travel and Tourism Press, Tel. 757181 x322: Beijing Branch: switchboard, tel. 757181.
For ticket information call CITS, Beijing Branch, 2 Qianmen Dong Ave., Tel. 755272.

Embassies

Australia, 15 Tungchimenwai. Tel. 522331.
United Kingdom, 11 Kwanghua lu. Tel. 521961.
Canada, 10 Sanlitun Rd. Tel. 521475.
New Zealand, 11 Second St., Ritan. Tel. 522731.
U.S.A., 17 Kwanghua lu. Tel. 522033.

HOTELS. There are a number of hotels in Beijing catering to foreign visitors. Some have been constructed recently while others have been accommodating guests for decades.

BEIJING HOTEL. The Beijing Hotel is the best known hotel in China. It adjoins the old French "Hotel de Pekin" (now used almost exclusively for local Chinese visitors to the capital).

The hotel has large but sparsely furnished salons, wide corridors, and gilt columns. The modern east wing is 16 stories high and has 910 rooms. The east wing room rate varies from ¥55 (single room: two beds), to ¥125–250 for a suite.

There are three outside telephone numbers for the hotel: 552231, 556531, 558331. If you wish to make a call from the hotel, dial "0" for an outside line; local calls are free of charge in Beijing. Dial extension 5199 or 4199 for trunk calls and Beijing telephone numbers; the operator speaks some English. For any telephone problems, dial 7199. There is also a telex (outgoing only).

The rooms are spacious, many with a balcony, and many overlook Chang An Boulevard, providing a panorama of the city. The rooms at the western end overlook the Forbidden City and Tien An Men Square (room numbers ending in 36, 37, 38, 39, 41, 43, 44).

The hotel provides a full range of services and facilities for the tourist and visiting business executive. You will find restaurants, bank, post and telegraph office, arts and crafts shop, food shop, ladies' hairdressing salon, and gentlemen's hairdresser. There is also a good antique shop on the first floor.

The main dining room is located on the lobby floor to the right on entering the hotel. This restaurant provides a Chinese and Western menu and caters to nonresident visitors as well as hotel guests. The mealtimes in the main dining room are as follows: breakfast, 7–8:30 A.M.; lunch, 12–2 P.M.; dinner, 6–8:30 P.M. On the second floor you will also find a Japanese restaurant, but reservations must be made in advance. There are private banquet rooms also located on the second floor. There is also a Sichuan-style restaurant.

CHANG CHENG HOTEL. The Chang Cheng, or Great Wall, Hotel, comprising three square-shouldered, glass-encased wings, provides the most luxurious accommodations available in Beijing. Located at North Donghuan Road near the Agricultural Exhibition Center, the Chang Cheng has an atrium six stories high, a cocktail lounge on the top floor, a French restaurant, a nightclub, a ballroom capable of seating 1,200 people, and a theater. The hotel is about a 20 minute drive from the center of Beijing, and about 35 minutes from the airport. Room rates begin at ¥140 for a single, rising to ¥350 for a suite.

YANJING HOTEL. The twenty-two story Yanjing Hotel is located just outside the Fuxingmen Gate, at 19 Fu Wai Street. The hotel comprises four buildings providing accommodations for 1,200 guests in 437 standard rooms, 19 deluxe rooms, and 59 suites; there are 19 meeting rooms. The standard service facilities are provided: restaurants, post office, exchange counter, shops, hairdressing salons, massage parlors, a luggage storeroom. Tel. 868721

The Chinese dining room has a huge mural—*The Light of Wisdom*—18 meters in length, depicting in acrylic various aspects of Chinese art. On the first floor there is a glazed ceramic fresco called *The Silk Road,* depicting merchants from all over the world coming to trade in Tang Dynasty China. The work was designed by three artists of the Beijing Central Institute of Arts and Crafts. All rooms are air conditioned (not sufficiently) and possess color television sets. Room rates vary from ¥120–150 for a suite.

JIANGUO HOTEL. This 7-story, 445-room hotel located at Jianguomenwai, a block and a half from the Friendship Store, was only recently constructed. The hotel possesses modern facilities in keeping with international standards, e.g., all rooms have individual air conditioning, stocked refrigerator, touch-dial telephone; coffee shops; bars; pool; disco. The restaurants are located on the top three floors: Justine's Grill Room (Western cuisine); Four Seasons Restaurant (Guangdong cuisine). Charlie's Cocktail Lounge is a popular place. The hotel is run as a joint-venture with the Peninsula Group of Hong Kong; as a consequence the standard of service is high. A number of foreign companies, particularly banks, have their offices in the hotel. Tel. 595261; 593661. Telex 22439 JGHBJ CN.

XIN QIAO HOTEL (pronounced "Shin Chow"), tel. 557731, is a gray-brick six-story building with a green-glazed tile roof. The hotel is only a few minutes' walk from Chang An Boulevard and is located in the interesting old "legation" quarter of Beijing.

Room rates are ¥40 per day for a standard room. The hotel provides a full range of services and facilities for the tourist and visiting business executive.

There is even a massage service available, but you must keep all your clothes on, although you are not expected to wear a hat during the head massage.

Coffee Shop: On the sixth floor; serves coffee, ice-cream sodas, pastries, and even martinis; closes at 11:30 P.M.

Restaurants: The Xin Qiao Hotel has two restaurants; the main one serving Chinese food is located on the ground floor—as you enter the lobby, go straight ahead and down a few steps. There is another dining room serving Western dishes located on the seventh floor. This restaurant also specializes in Pakistani food. The hours are the same in both: breakfast, 7–9 A.M.; lunch, 12 noon–2 P.M.; dinner, 6–9 P.M. The restaurants are also open to guests who are not residents of the hotel.

The hotel has the usual service facilities: shops, post office, bank, hairdressing salons, and billiards room. Taxis may be ordered at the taxi desk in the lobby.

MINZU HOTEL, or Nationalities Hotel, is housed in a yellow brick building located off the main West Chang An Avenue. It is about seven minutes by car from Tien An Men Square, the center of Beijing. Tel. 668541; 668761.

At press time, the Minzu is being refurbished and is expected to re-open in 1985.

There are two restaurants located on the ground floor. The one on the right of the entrance serves Chinese food and the one on the left Western food. The hours are the same in both: breakfast, 7–9 A.M.; lunch, 12 noon–2 P.M.; dinner, 6–9 P.M. The restaurants are also open to guests who are not residents of the hotel.

The hotel has various shops, a post office, bank, hairdressing salons, and billiard room. Taxis may be ordered at the taxi desk in the lobby.

QIANMEN HOTEL. The Front Gate Hotel (tel. 338731) is an old building providing 170-room accommodations. Located in what was once the Chinese Outer City, near the Qianmen and Mao Zedong Mausoleum, this hotel is well situated for strolling in areas of Beijing that hold a fascination for foreign visitors. It is only one kilometer from the antique shops (Liulichang), busy shopping streets, restaurants, and old-style houses (see section on Beijing "Atmosphere"). However, the hotel's facilities are not all up to standard: some rooms do not have a bath or telephone; the range of goods in the lobby shop is limited; and the food is only average. Room rates are ￥35–50 (single).

XIYUAN HOTEL. The Western Garden Hotel (tel. 890721), located in Xizhimenwai Rd. near the Zoo and the Planetarium, has a pleasant setting in quiet surroundings. A new wing has been added providing 756 rooms. The usual service facilities are available. The restaurant is passable, but some rooms in the old wing do not have a bath or a telephone. However, the hotel has the advantage of being near the Temple of the Five Pagodas, Purple Bamboo Park, and the Temple of the White Dagoba. Room rates are ￥40–70 (single).

FRIENDSHIP HOTEL, or Youyi Binguan (tel. 890621), a gray-brick building with a traditional green-tiled Chinese roof, is located in the northwestern district of Beijing. It is a fair way from the city and takes about twenty minutes by car from the center. The hotel has a number of buildings set on large grounds, the main building being six stories high. The southern blocks have flats to accommodate some of the foreign residents and their families working in Beijing. The hotel was originally built in the early 50's to accommodate the thousands of Soviet technicians who were sent to provide technical assistance to China.

Rooms cost ￥40 per day for a standard room accommodating two.

The dining room serves breakfast 7–8:30 A.M., lunch, noon–1:30 P.M., and dinner, 6–8 P.M. It is available to hotel guests only. There is a large banquet hall along the corridor from the main dining room which can seat up to 120 guests. Across from this room there are two lounge rooms which may be used for the customary tea-drinking before or after the banquet.

An attraction of this hotel is its outdoor swimming pool, open from June through September, and tennis courts. There is even a dance hall which is sometimes used as a disco. The standard services of post office, foreign exchange counter, shops, hairdressers, billiards, and table-tennis are available.

The main disadvantage of the hotel is its distance from the city. However, the hotel runs a shuttle bus service to the center of Beijing.

XIANGSHAN HOTEL. Known as the Fragrant Hills Hotel (tel. 819242) because of its location in the Western region of Beijing, this superb hotel was designed by Chinese-American architect I. M. Pei. There is a magnificent atrium; swimming pool; health club with sauna; 313 rooms, all with modern facilities. The hotel suffers the disadvantage of being some distance from the center of Beijing; however this is balanced by the peaceful countryside and the easier access to the major sites located to the northwest and northeast of Beijing. Rates range from ￥120 (single) to ￥240 (suite).

HUAQIAO HOTEL. This hotel (tel. 558851) caters to overseas Chinese visitors. Located on the corner of Wangfujing and East Dongsi Streets, it is in the very center of the city. Another 6 floors have been added providing an additional 530-room accommodation.

OTHER HOTELS. Airport hotel (tel. 52.29.31), located at Beijing International Airport, is often used by travelers taking early-morning flights. **Huadu Hotel** in the Sanlitun area of Beijing is frequently used by tour groups. Other hotel possibilities include **Heping** (Peace); **Yanxiang; Bei Wei; Bamboo Gardens** (Zhu Yuan); **Diaoyutai Guest House; Dongfeng; Jingxi; Xiangyang No. 1** and **No. 2.**

DINING OUT. China offers the visitor wonderful opportunities to become acquainted with one of the highly developed aspects of its civilization; the exquisite preparation of food. When you visit Beijing you will carry away memories of sumptuous banquets where the dishes are nothing short of magnificent.

Not unexpectedly, the restaurants of Beijing specialize mainly in the northern or Pekinese style of cooking. This style has evolved over the centuries: from the Moslem Chinese, from the traditions of the Lower Yangzi River area, and from the cuisine developed in the Old Imperial Palace of the Qing Dynasty.

Northern or Pekinese cooking tends to be oilier (e.g., Peking roast duck) and the dishes saltier and spicier than other styles. The northern style alone uses lamb, a characteristic borrowed from Chinese Moslem cooking. Wheat and other grains in the form of dumplings, noodles, and buns are standard fare at northern Chinese meals. Moslem-Chinese restaurants invariably feature roasting, barbecuing, and deep-boiling techniques.

There are only a handful of restaurants in Beijing devoted to eastern, central-western and southern cooking and, outside of hotels, you will be hard put to find a Cantonese restaurant worthy of the name. Most restaurants with banquet rooms cook in the Hebei, Shandong, or Moslem-Chinese style.

The restaurants of Beijing are noted for their austere surroundings, lack of decoration, and subdued ambiance. There are generally no distractions to take your mind off the superb dishes. Two restaurants are exceptions: the Fang Shan in Bei Hai Park and the Sichuan Restaurant. Both have magnificent decors.

Of course, there are several thousand "masses'" restaurants in Peking which are patronized by the locals and, having no private rooms, cannot cope with a large number of foreign guests with what would be considered appropriate courtesy. If you wish to visit a masses' restaurant you will need to speak Chinese or have someone in your party who does, and there should not be more than four or five people in your group, or it will be difficult for the restaurant to seat you without causing too much fuss or inconvenience to the other patrons.

Generally speaking, the food served at the masses' restaurants is simple but quite nutritious. However, you should be warned that their hygiene is probably suspect by the standards of the West.

Banquet costs vary considerably from one restaurant to another. A price of ¥25 per person is standard at less prestigious restaurants. At one of the top flight restaurants a minimum of ¥50 should be expected. You can make reservations at any of the restaurants catering to foreigners by getting your hotel to make the arrangements. The restaurant will expect you to advise the cost per person and the number of guests.

If you prefer to eat western food, there are a number of restaurants providing such meals.

THE TOP TEN RESTAURANTS OF BEIJING

The following list is not in order of rank except for the top three. There is little doubt that the finest food in Beijing is served in the Feng Ze Yuan, the Fang Shan in Bei Hai Park, and the Sichuan Restaurant. However, while the restaurant serving the banquet rooms (not the general dining rooms) of the Beijing Hotel provides magnificent food, it has been considered separately in this review; the "top ten" list comprises restaurants that are not located in hotels.

In the section, "Recommended Banquet Menus," the Beijing Hotel Restaurant is listed after the "Fang Shan." This particular banquet menu is undoubtedly the finest of the ones listed in this book. The dishes make up a superb banquet and would be suitable for a dinner given in honor of top-level visitors or for a farewell dinner for your Chinese hosts.

Address	Restaurant	Style	Telephone
Feng Ze Yuan 183 Zhushikou St. (West)	Garden of Abundance and Color (or "Horn of Plenty")	Northern Chinese Shandong	332828
Fang Shan Bei Hai Park	Dining on a Boat Rest.	Northern Chinese and Imperial Court	442573
Sichuan 51 West Rong Xian Lane	Sichuan Province Restaurant	Central/Western	336356
Cui Hua Lou 60 Wang Fu Jing	Capital Restaurant	Northern Chinese (Shandong)	554581
Jin Yang 241 Zhushikou St. (West)	Sunny Shanxi Restaurant	Northern Chinese (Shanxi)	334361 331669 332120
Huai Yang Fan Zhuang 217 Xi Dan Bei Dajie	Huai Yang Style Restaurant	Eastern Chinese (Jiangsu; Zhejiang)	660521
Kang Le 259 An Ding Men Nei Dajie	Happiness and Enjoyment Restaurant	Southern Border (Yunnan)	443884
Qing Hai Dongsibeidajie 555	Qinghai Province Restaurant	North Western Chinese	442947
Tong He Ju 3 Xi Si Nan Dajie	Peace and Harmony Restaurant	Northern Chinese (Shandong)	660925
Zhen Jiang Hsun Nei Dajie	City of Zhen Jiang Restaurant	Eastern Chinese (Jiangsu; Shanghai)	662115 662289

The Great Hall of the People has opened a restaurant. It serves a range of traditional Chinese dishes prepared in Northern, Cantonese, Jiangsu, Shandong, and Sichuan styles. If you would like to eat there ask your CITS guide or hotel to make a reservation.

THREE BEIJING BANQUETS

Your tour program will probably be full, with not much spare time available. For this reason you may need some guidance on the restaurants to visit in Beijing in the restricted time at your disposal.

If you have time for only three banquets—and keep in mind that these can be lunches or dinners—you should perhaps give priority to restaurants on the following list.

Restaurant	Style	Telephone
Feng Ze Yuan (Garden of Abundance & Color) 183 Zhushikou St. (West)	Shandong	332828
Fang Shan Bei Hai Lake and Park	Northern Chinese (Peking) and Imperial Court	442573
Sichuan 51 West Rong Xian Lane	Central/Western (Sichuan)	336356

Consult the section "Recommended Banquet Menus" for advice on the dishes for your banquet and for a description of some of the specialties.

FOUR BEIJING BANQUETS

If you are fortunate enough to have a longer period in Beijing, or more free time than is usual, you may wish to try four banquets.

The list of restaurants presented below has been selected so that you can experience a wide variety of Chinese cooking styles.

Restaurant	Style	Telephone
Feng Ze Yuan (Garden of Abundance & Color) 183 Zhushikou St. (West)	Shandong	332828
Fang Shan Bei Hai Lake and Park	Northern Chinese (Beijing) and Imperial Court	442573
Beijing Kao Ya Dian (The "Sick Duck") 13 Wang Fuxing	Northern Chinese (Peking Duck)	553310
Sichuan 51 West Rong Xian Lane	Central/Western (Sichuan)	336356

The list selects the three top restaurants of Beijing (Feng Ze Yuan, Fang Shan, and Sichuan), and the best roast duck restaurant (The "Sick Duck").

You could replace the "Sick Duck" with the "Big Duck" (Qian Men Kao Ya Dian) without loss of quality or style, as they are branches of the same restaurant. So too is the "Super Duck" or Heping Kao Ya Dian. For more details consult the section on "Peking Roast Duck Restaurants" that follows and the "Recommended Banquet Menus" section.

PEKING ROAST DUCK RESTAURANTS

Everyone visiting Beijing wishes to try Peking roast duck, a dish with a reputation throughout the world. In a sense it is a misnomer to call it a dish because, at the famous roast duck restaurants in Beijing, it is served as a series of dishes, most parts of the duck being consumed. Of course, other dishes are served between the duck courses to add variety to the banquet.

In the section on recommended menus the ones selected for the duck restaurants feature banquets where most courses are duck. However, it is possible to eat Peking roast duck as only one or two courses. Indeed some people prefer this, so you will find roast duck on the suggested menus for a number of restaurants which do not actually specialize in its preparation.

There are a number of top restaurants in Beijing specializing in roast duck. The best known is the Peking Roast Duck Restaurant (Beijing Kao Ya Dian), known to residents of the city as the "Sick Duck" because the restaurant is located in a small lane off Wang Fu Jing leading to the Capital Hospital. This endearing name easily distinguishes it from the duck restaurant located in Qian Men, known as the "Big Duck."

The "Big Duck" is really a sister restaurant of the Peking Duck restaurant; it is more brightly lit and less subdued in atmosphere and therefore less liked by some. There is no difference, however, in the quality of the food served.

Then there is the "Super Duck" restaurant, so called because of its size. It is the largest Peking Duck restaurant in the world. Situated near Hepingmen in a seven-story building, its 41 dining halls of various sizes can seat 2,500. Some foreign residents refer to it as "McDonald Duck."

Of course you can eat Peking Duck menus in the major hotels, perhaps the best one being the Zhongwenmenwai Kaoyadian, situated in the new Zhongwenmenwai St., tel. 75-05-05.

Restaurant	Telephone
Beijing Kao Ya Dian, or Peking Roast Duck Restaurant 13 Wang Fu Jing (The "Sick Duck")	553310
Qian Men Kao Ya Dian, or Qian Men Roast Duck Restaurant 32 Qian Men Dajie (The "Big Duck")	751379
Heping Kao Ya Dian or Peace Gate Roast Duck Restaurant Xianwu, Hepingmen (The "Super Duck" or "McDonald Duck")	338031

"HIDEAWAY" RESTAURANTS

One problem a group visitor to China faces is how to get away from organized activity for a while and simply be alone. For this reason we list a few "hideaway" restaurants where two people can easily slip away for a quiet meal. They are:

Kao Rou Ji, or "Season for Roasting" Restaurant, 14 Chienhai Dong Yen. Tel. 445921.

Dong Lai Shun or "Favorable East Wind" Rest. (formerly the Min Zu Fan Zhuang, or "Nationality" Restaurant), Jinyu Hutung (North entrance of Dong Feng Market off Wang Fu Jing). Tel. 550069.

Ri Tan Gong Yuan, or *"Temple of the Sun Park" Restaurant,* Ri Tan Park. Tel. 592648.

The *Kou Rou Ji* is a delightful little place, quiet, unpretentious, and the only spot in Beijing where you can dine on a balcony overlooking a lake. It is surrounded by small Chinese houses set in tiny lanes, and in the evenings you can see the Chinese sitting indoors under a dim light, gathered around a table eating, playing cards, or reading. It is rare to get so close. You will hear the chatter of the people below and children playing or singing well-known Chinese songs.

The restaurant cannot compare with those on the top ten list but nevertheless serves an excellent meal. You must book in advance, and a recommended banquet menu has been provided. As the name suggests, it prepares food in Mongolian style and therefore features barbecues and roasted meats. You will probably need a minimum of four in your party.

The *Dong Lai Shun* is only a short walk (ten minutes) from the Peking Hotel and therefore very convenient for many visitors. One advantage is that you can sometimes book a table on short notice, but probably 6 P.M. would be the latest you could hope to arrange a dinner. This restaurant cooks in Mongolian style, and some residents feel that it provides the best Mongolian hot pot in all of Beijing. A booking for two people can be made, so it is ideal for those seeking a little privacy.

The *Temple of the Sun Park* restaurant is seldom visited by tourists because of its unusual location. It is situated in the Ri Tan Park, about 250 yards from the Beijing Friendship Store. You cannot enter the park by taxi, so on arriving at the main entrance go down the main walk, then follow the red wall of the old sacrificial ground as it curves to the right. About 100 yards along the path by the wall you will see to your right an entrance leading into a walled court-yard. Inside are two well-restored traditional Chinese pavilions, one of which houses the restaurant.

The restaurant is excessively lit and unattractive, but the food though simple is good. Some residents feel that the *jiao zi* (something like dumplings) are the best in Beijing; the sauteed pepper shrimp are also worth trying. The restaurant is unusual in that you cannot book dishes ahead or reserve a table. It is closed on Fridays.

MONGOLIAN STYLE RESTAURANTS

Two of the restaurants serving food cooked in the Mongolian style have been reviewed in the previous section. They are:

Dong Lai Shun, or *"Favorable East Wind Restaurant"* (formerly the Minzu Fan Zhuang or "Nationalities Restaurant"), Jinyu Hutung. Tel. 55.00.69.

Kou Rou Ji, 133 Xi Dan Bei Dajie ("Season for Roasting Restaurant"). Tel. 44.59.21.

Another worth trying is *Kou Rou Wan, 102 Xun Nei Dajie* ("Roasted Meat Restaurant"). Tel. 33.07.00.
A charming place; you can cook your own meat on barbecue skewers.

An interesting restaurant specializing in Mongolian food is located in the Palace of National Minorities: *Chang An Dajie.* Tel. 66.72.68. Because all the food must be ordered in advance, enlist the aid of your hotel staff or guide if you cannot speak Chinese. A good, standard menu is: cold hors d'oeuvres, shaslik, Mongolian hot pot, sesame buns, jiaozi, noodles, fruits (particularly honey melon, or "hami gua," in season).

PORK RESTAURANTS

Sha Guo Ju, 60 Xisinandajie. Tel. 661126. Known as the "Restaurant of the Ceramic Cooking Pots"; it is famous for its pork dishes, the only meat served. It is also the oldest restaurant in Beijing, existing for over 300 years.

OTHER RESTAURANTS SERVING CHINESE MEALS

If you have not booked a restaurant yet you feel like eating Chinese food, you can eat à la carte at the following

Beijing Hotel, Chang An Dajie. Tel. 556531
Xin Qiao Hotel, Fan Di Lu. Tel. 557731
Min Zu Hotel, West Chang An Dajie. Tel. 668541
International Club, Qien Guo Men Wai (closed Mondays). Tel. 552144
San Li Tun Restaurant, San Li Tun Diplomatic Office Building. Tel. 521007

All the above establishments have banquet rooms as well. As indicated earlier, the meals served in the Peking Hotel banquet rooms are among the finest in all Beijing. However, do not expect the food in the vast general dining room to match this standard.

The Chinese restaurant of the Xin Qiao is on the ground floor of the hotel. The standard is good, certainly better than the Peking Hotel dining hall.

The other three—the Min Zu Hotel, the International Club, and the San Li Tun Restaurant—maintain a reasonable standard but lack any distinctive features.

RESTAURANTS OUTSIDE BEIJING

The *Ting Li Guan* (tel. 281936) is located inside the grounds of the Summer Palace on the northern shore of the lake and at the foot of the manmade Hill of Longevity. The name means "Pavilion for Listening to Birds Sing," and the restaurant is housed in a number of magnificently restored Chinese pavilions with traditional glazed tile roofs and ornately decorated columns and interior walls.

The restaurant is excellent and expensive; specialties are fish from the Summer Palace Lake, prawns, and deep-fried *jiao zi.*

You should reserve in advance; it is a long way from Beijing (three-quarters of an hour by car), and if you take a chance you may find the restaurant booked up.

The *Fragrant Hills Restaurant* (tel. 819244) is located in Beijing's famous Western Hills district. It is a favorite place for Beijing foreign residents, who like to get away from the city on weekends and stroll among the beautiful hills. The more energetic who climb the peak often order their meal on the way up so that it will be ready upon their return. The restaurant probably has the best spring rolls in Beijing. You should book in advance on weekends.

RESTAURANTS SERVING WESTERN FOOD

Perhaps you do not care for Chinese food, or maybe you have already eaten a great deal of it on your tour and are looking forward to a Western meal. All of the new hotels of international standard have Western dining rooms and coffee shops. The most prominent are: *Chang Cheng* (Great Wall), *Jianguo*, and the *Xiang Shan*. However, should you prefer to try Western food prepared in the older Chinese establishments, then one of the following may suit:

Xin Qiao Hotel, Fan Di Lu. Tel: 557731. Probably the best western restaurant in Beijing; service usually good. It is on the sixth floor.

"Russian" Restaurant, Exhibition Hall, or Peking Exhibition Center Restaurant. Tel: 893713. Good steaks; Russian-style food may be ordered, hence the name. Caviar (red and black) particularly good. Overlooks the zoo.

Beijing Hotel, Chang An Dajie. Tel: 556531. Ask for the Western menu. Some suggest that the food looks western but tastes Chinese. Service varies from rude to humorously bad. It is trying to improve, and there is plenty of room for progress.

Min Zu Hotel, or "Nationalities" Hotel, West Chang An Dajie. Tel: 668541. The western dining room is on the left as you enter. Reasonable standards. The Baked Alaska is excellent.

International Club, Qien Guo Men Wai (closed Mondays). Tel: 552144. Fairly limited Western menu. Best dishes are chicken à la Kiev, prawn fritters, pork skewer, prawns in butter sauce, cheese soufflé, chocolate soufflé (very sweet). It is interesting to watch the diplomats eating.

San Li Tun, San Li Tun Diplomatic Office Building. Tel: 521007. Very limited Western menu and often tastes like Chinese food anyway. Not really recommended unless you happen to collapse from hunger nearby.

"MASSES" RESTAURANTS

"Masses" restaurants are where the Chinese people eat. They are usually small, crowded, and limited in their menu, so be prepared for simple fare. There are no menus written in English so you will have to point at the dishes being served to others, unless you have a Chinese speaker in the party.

"Masses" restaurants are not for everyone. For one thing their hygiene is suspect. The chopsticks and bowls are sometimes greasy and poorly washed. The cement floors are often littered with scraps, gristle, small bones. In some areas you run the risk of exposing yourself to hepatitis and tuberculosis. However, the ones listed below are better than most yet will still provide you with a glimpse of how the ordinary person eats.

At the top end is the *Yangjing Restaurant*, located adjacent to the Yangjing Hotel in Fuxingmen Avenue (No. 19). *Dongfeng Market Restaurant*, located on Jinyu (Goldfish) Hutung off Wangfujing, is more typical of the "masses" type, although it stays open 24 hours a day. *Shanxi Noodle Restaurant*, on Doinganmen Road, near the northern end of Wangfujing. *The Duyichu Shaomai Restaurant* is located at 36 Qianmen Road.

RECOMMENDED BANQUET MENUS

FENG ZE YUAN

丰泽园 — Garden of Selected Abundance or Horn of Plenty

珠市口西大街183号 — 183 Zhushikou Street (West)

电话：332828 — Telephone: 33.28.28

Northern Chinese Cooking
(Shandong)

Feng Ze Yuan is probably the best restaurant in Beijing and is therefore one of the foremost Chinese restaurants in the world. However, its decor lacks distinction. If you are a gourmet, or even someone who simply likes Chinese food, you should take the opportunity to indulge yourself here. By choosing carefully you can eat inexpensively at this prestigious restaurant, but obviously if you order many of the rare and exquisite delicacies you can expect to pay accordingly.

The menu presented below is suitable for 5 people and would cost about Y45 per person, not including drinks.

Chinese	Pinyin	English
冷 盘	Lěng pán	Assorted Hors d'Oeuvres
鸡蓉鱼翅	Jīróng yúchì	Chicken Puffs with Sharksfin
香酥鸭	Xiāngsū yā	Crisp Duck
大 虾	Dà xiā	Prawns
龙须菜	Lóngxūcai	Asparagus
鸡 丁	Jī dīng	Diced Chicken
红烧鱼	Hóngshāo yú	Braised Fish in Brown Sauce
点 心	Diǎnxīn	Dessert
汤	Tāng	Soup (with Cuttlefish Eggs)
拔丝萍果	Básī Píngguǒ	Caramelized Apples

A specialty of the restaurant is Chicken Puffs with Sharksfin. This dish consists of chopped white chicken meat with whipped eggwhite cooked with sharksfin in chicken stock.

Another special dish is the *Hongshao Yu*, which is a fish cooked in a dark soy sauce. The fish is served in the rich brown sauce, the ingredients being mainly ginger, chili pepper, sugar, and scallion.

Since you may wish to try the Feng Ze Yuan again during your stay, a second banquet menu has been selected; it is of comparable quality, would cost about ¥35 per person not including drinks, and is suitable for 7–10 people.

Chinese	Pinyin	English
拼四样	Pīsiyàng	Hors d'Oeuvres
鸡蓉鱼翅	Jīróng Yúchì	Chicken Puffs with Sharksfin
炸鸭肝	Zhá yāgān	Deep Fried Duck Liver
鸡油鲜蘑茭白	Jīyóu siānmó jiāobái	Mushrooms and Vegetable Shoots in Chicken Fat
雪花大虾	Xǔe huā dàxiā	Snowflake Prawns
香酥鸡	Xiāngsū jī	Crisp Fried Chicken
炒生鸡片鲜椒	Chǎo shēng jī piàn xiānjiāo	Sauté Diced Chicken with Green Chili
烩乌龟蛋	Wūguēi dàn	Stewed Cuttlefish Eggs
冰镇果羹	Bīng zhèn gǔogēng	Fruit Jelly

SICHUAN RESTAURANT

西绒线胡同51号   51 West Rong Xian Lane

电话：336356   Telephone: 33.63.56

Central/Western Chinese Cooking
(Sichuan)

The Sichuan Restaurant is one of the three prestigious restaurants of Beijing and without a doubt has the finest setting of any restaurant in the capital.

Sichuan is a central province of China noted for its abundant food production and a population which favors hot and spicy food. The dishes served at the restaurant in Beijing reflect this preference, but, as is usual with a Chinese banquet, there is always a fine balance among dishes that create different effects on the palate.

The menu presented below is suitable for 15–20 people and would cost about ¥45 per person, not including drinks.

Chinese	Pinyin	English
冷　盘	Lěng pán	Cold Hors d'Oeuvres
鸡兰鱼翅	Jīlán yúchì	Sharksfin with Chicken and Bamboo Shoots
米熏子鸡	Mǐxūn zǐjī	Chicken Cooked in Red Wine
荷叶饼	Héyè bǐng	Meats Wrapped in Lotus Leaf
鲜蘑时菜	Xiānmó shícaì	Mushrooms and Fresh Vegetables
鱼香大虾	Yúxiāng dàxiā	Sichuan Prawns
大肚鸭脯	Dàràng yāfǔ	Stuffed Duck Breast
干烧青鱼	Gānshāo qīngyú	Fish in Chili Sauce
菠罗捞糟	Bōlúo láozao	Pineapples Marinated in Rice Wine
园汤素烩	Yuántāng sùhùi	Soup with Vegetable Chowder

The specialty in this menu is Sichun prawns, which are the famous large prawns sauteed in soy sauce and vinegar, garlic, ginger, and chili. Not unexpectedly, this is a hot, spicy dish, typical of those derived from this region. The literal translation of the Chinese for this dish is Prawn with Fish Fragrance.

Another specialty of the restaurant is Sharksfin with Chicken and Bamboo Shoots.

As the Sichuan Restaurant is one of the foremost restaurants of Beijing, you may wish to dine there again during your stay. A second selected banquet menu is provided below; it is of the same excellent quality as the first but, because the menu caters for a greater number of guests, it has more courses.

The banquet would be suitable for 15–25 persons at about ¥45 per person, not including drinks.

Chinese	Pinyin	English
冷　盘	Lěng pán	Cold Hors d'Oeuvres
热　菜	Rè caì	Hot Dish
鸡兰鱼翅	Jī lán yú chì	Chicken with Sharksfin
樟茶鸭子	Zhāng chá yāzi	Smoked Duck with Camphor and Tea Leaves

Chinese	Pinyin	English
兰笋瑶蛀	Lán cǔn yaozhu	Bamboo Shoots with Dried Scallops
鱼香大虾	Yú xiāng dàxiā	Prawns with Fish Flavor
花仁子鸡	Huā rén zǐ jī	Chicken with Peanuts
干烧青鱼	Gān shāo qīng yú	Fish in Hot Sauce
凉 面	Liáng miàn	Cold Noodles
竹笋鲜蘑汤	Zhū sǔn xiān mó tāng	Soup with Bamboo Sprouts and Fresh Mushrooms
冰汁凉桃脯	Bīng zhē liáng táo fǔ	Iced Fresh Peach Slices
水 果	Shǔi guǒ	Fresh Fruits

A well-known dish in this menu is Chicken with Peanuts, which will be familiar to those who have dined at one of the many Sichuan restaurants in New York. Try it under authentic circumstances in the capital of China, and see how it compares.

FANG SHAN RESTAURANT

仿膳饭庄	Dining on a Boat Restaurant (lit. "Same Food" Rest.)
北海公园	Bei Hai Lake and Park
电话: 442573	Telephone: 44.25.73

Northern Chinese (Beijing) and
Imperial Court Style

The Fang Shan, located on Qiong Hua Island in the Bei Hai Lake, is the most beautiful restaurant in Beijing and highly sought after as a place for banquets.

Enter Bei Hai Lake and Park by the southeast gate (main entrance). Turn to the right and cross the bridge to the island. Take the path to the right and follow it along the shoreline. You will pass the Bridge of Perfect Wisdom on your right and finally enter the "covered way," similar to the one at the Summer Palace. Note the beautifully painted cross-members and ceiling.

As the corridor curves to the left you will notice the Pavilion of the Five Dragons on the opposite shore. The corridor separates a group of fan-shaped buildings from the lake and then opens up into an ancient pavilion which is now the restaurant.

Inside there are courtyards opening through moon gates into other courtyards, the dining rooms flanking them on all sides.

The following menu is suitable for 8–10 guests and costs ¥55 per person, not including drinks.

CHINESE	ENGLISH
五冷荤	Five Cold Hors d'Oeuvres
扒三白	Stewed Three Whites
荷包软炸大虾	Prawns en Chemise
琥珀鸽蛋	Amber Glazed Quail Eggs
青椒鸡	Green Peppered Chicken
锅烧鸡	Whole Roasted Capon
干烧活鱼	Spicy Whole Fish
鸡油扁豆	Snow Peas Sauteed in Chicken Fat
肉末烧饼	Minced Pork Stuffed in Sesame Buns
清汤竹笋	Vegetable Consomme
冷热点心	Cold Desserts—Hot Desserts
水果	Fresh Fruit

Stewed Three Whites is a form of soup containing bamboo shoots, fish maw, mushrooms, and their juices. *Spicy Whole Fish* is prepared from fish freshly caught in the Bei Hai Lake outside the restaurant. *Minced Pork Stuffed in Sesame Buns* may sound commonplace, but it is a delicious dish of minced pork, flavored with herbs. The minced meat is stuffed into sesame buns. The *Cold Dessert* in this menu consists of small red-and-white bean paste cakes, favorites of the last Dowager Empress. One of the better known and delicious hot desserts is *Almond Cream Soup*, prepared with freshly ground almonds.

Two remarkable dishes not included in the above menu of this restaurant are the rare and famous *Camel's Hump* and *Bear's Paws*. You can order a banquet at the Fang Shan that includes these delicacies, but the dining experience will set you back ¥75–100 per person or more.

Note: This restaurant must be booked at least four to five days in advance for dinner as it is used extensively by the Chinese ministries and corporations for entertaining foreign guests. If you wish to dine at Fang Shan, you should reserve a table as soon as possible after you arrive in Beijing.

Another menu, more modest in price and quality than the one above, is suitable as a lunch for 4–6 people. It would cost about ¥35 per person, not including drinks.

Chinese	English
拼　盘	Cold Hors d'Oeuvres
罗汉大虾	Lo Han Giant Prawns
溜鸡脯	Silky Chicken Breast
清蒸鱼	Steamed Fish from Bei Hai Lake
鸡油菜心	Green Vegetables in Chicken Stock
炒肉末烧饼	Sauteed Pork with Sesame Buns
清汤竹笋	Mushroom and Bamboo Shoots Soup
冷热点心	Hot Dian Xin (hot dumplings) Cold Sweet Desserts

The Lo Han Giant Prawns are served in two styles: split prawns under chopped prawn balls in aspic, and in the shells in a soy and ginger sauce.

The *dim sum* (called *dian xin* in Mandarin) are excellent, the cold variety being a favorite dish of the last Empress of China.

BEIJING HOTEL RESTAURANT

北京饭店	Beijing Fandian or **Beijing** Hotel Restaurant
长安大街	Chang An Da Jie
电话：556531	Telephone: 55.65.31

Northern Chinese Cooking
(Beijing)

The menu presented below is suitable for 25 people and would cost about ¥75 per person, not including drinks. It is a superb menu and without doubt the finest of the Beijing selection. If you wish to repay the kindness of your Chinese hosts, there is no better way than to invite them to a banquet similar to the one given below.

Chinese	Pinyin	English
冷菜类	[Lěng cài lèi]	[Cold Dishes]
桂花鸭子	Guìhūa yāzi	Cassia Flower Duck
蚝油白鸡	Háoyóu báijī	Chicken in Oyster Sauce
叉烧肉	Chashāo ròu	Grilled Pork
虾菜拌兔丝	Xiācai bàntùsī	Tossed Rabbit Slices and Bean Sprouts
介目鸭掌	Jiè mù yāzhǎng	Mustard Duck Webfoot
三色黄瓜卷	Sānsī huángguā juǎn	Three Shreds and Stuffed Cucumber Rolls
鸡油冬菇	Jīyóu dōnggū	Black Mushrooms in Chicken Fat
茄汁鱼片	Qié zhī yúpiàn	Fish Slices in Tomato Sauce
油浸鲜蘑	Yóujìn xiānmó	Marinated Mushrooms
	[Rè cài]	[Hot Dishes]
鸟鹌蛋鲍鱼	Yānguō dàn bāoyú	Abalone and Quail Eggs
羊肉串	Yángròu chuàn	Lamb Shashliks
罐焖肉鸡	Guànmèn ròujī	Chicken Braised in Pot
鸡油龙须菜	Jīyóu lóngxūcài	Asparagus in Chicken Fat
蒸鲜鱼	Zhēng xiānyú	Steamed Fresh Fish
鲁酥鸭子	Lúsū yāzi	Crispy Duck
生片火锅	Shēngpiàn huǒguō	Hot Pot
	Diǎnsin	DESSERTS
冰糖银耳	Bīngtáng yíněr	Snow Mushrooms in Crystallized Sugar

It is impossible in a menu such as this to select one course as being more outstanding than another. The menu is superbly balanced.

You may wish to dine a second time at the Beijing Hotel banquet rooms, or perhaps order something more modest than the previous banquet; therefore a second menu is presented below. It is suitable for 10 people and would cost about ¥45 per person, not including drinks.

Chinese	Pinyin	English
冷 盘	Lěng pán	Cold Hors d'Oeuvres
清汤银耳	Qīng tāng yíněr	Consommé with Snow Mushrooms
鸡丝鱼翅	Jīsī yúchì	Sharksfin with Chicken Shreds
两吃大虾	Liǎngchī dàxiā	Prawns Cooked in Two Styles
鲜蘑尤菜	Xiānmó yóucài	Fresh Mushrooms with Vegetables
宫爆鸡丁	Gōngbào jīdīng	Diced Chicken with Chili Pepper
樟茶鸭子	Zhāngchá yāzi	Duck Smoked in Camphor Wood and Fragrant Tea Leaves
点心四样	Diǎnxīn sì yàng	Four Desserts
元 宵	Yuánxiāo	Yuan Xiao Cakes with Tangerine Flavor

One specialty is Sharksfin with Chicken Shreds. Another is Duck Smoked in Camphor Wood and Tea Leaves; as the name suggests, the duck is prepared by exposing it to the smoke of camphor wood and tea leaves, thus giving it its distinctive flavor and pink coloration. The dish is a specialty of northern and western China.

CUI HUA LOU (formerly SHOU DU)

萃苹楼   Luxuriant Place (formerly "Capital")

王府井大街六十号   60 Wang Fu Jing

电话：554581，   Telephone: 55.45.81

552594   55.25.94

Northern Chinese Cooking
(Shandong)

Shou Du simply means "capital," and this is certainly one of the finest restaurants in Beijing as the name would suggest.

The menu presented below is suitable for 4 persons and would cost about ¥40 per person, not including drinks.

Chinese	Pinyin	English
冷 盘	Lěng pán	Assorted Cold Hors d'Oeuvres
扒鱼翅	Pā yúchì	Grilled Sharksfin
桃花饭	Taóhuā fàn	Peach Flower Rice
炸大虾	Xhá dàxiā	Deep Fried Prawns
油淋子鸡	Yóulín sǔbjî	Oiled Chicken with Bamboo Shoots
干熠辣鱼段	Gānshaō là yúduàn	Fried Fish Slices with Chili
醋椒三鲜	Cùjiaō sānxiān	Three Vegetables in Hot and Sour Sauce
杏仁豆腐三果	Xìnrén doùfu sān gǔo	Almond Beancurd with Mixed Fruit

A specialty is the Chicken with Bamboo Shoots, which is something like a soup and suitable for eating with rice. The dish is made from shredded chicken breasts, shredded bamboo shoots, salt, ginger, and sherry. Other ingredients are egg white and flour. The chicken is cooked for only a very short time, and the result is a dish which is light and simple.

The Vegetables in Hot and Sour Sauce is another well-known dish. The sauce is made from chicken broth by adding salt, pepper, sherry, vinegar, coriander, sesame oil, and spring onions.

The specialty of the restaurant is Grilled Shark's fin. This dish is rare in China; shark's fin is usually served shredded, not in the form of whole pieces. Accordingly, when you order this dish you can expect a large bill at the end of the banquet.

The restaurant prepares a delightful dessert in the form of Almond Bean Curd with Mixed Fruit. Visitors from overseas who are familiar with Chinese food may have had this at their favorite Chinese restaurant, but it will have been prepared with almond-flavored gelatin instead of the freshly ground almond paste used in this first-class restaurant. Consequently the flavor and texture are richer.

The menu listed below is suitable for 10 people and would cost about ¥35 per person, not including drinks.

CHINESE	ENGLISH
四盖碗双拼	Four Platters of Double-Cold Hors d'Oeuvres
鸡油鲍鱼龙须玉蘑	Abalone and Mushroom with Chicken Fat
桃花泛	Plum Flower Ice
干炸虾鸭肝冬笋	Deep-Fried Duck Liver with Bamboo Shoots
口蘑烧四宝	Four Kinds of Treasures
点心 酥盒子 葱油饼	Breads: Multilayered Cakes Scallion Cakes
干烧辣目鱼	Whole Fish with Chili Sauce
山东烧笋鸡	Shandong Roast Capon
醋椒三鲜汤	Three Delicacy Soup—Ham, Chicken Slices, Pork
杏仁豆腐三果	Cold Almond Cream with Mixed Fruits

JIN YANG

晋阳饭店	Shanxi Restaurant
珠市口西大街241号	241 Zhu Shi Kou Street (West)
电话： 334361	Telephone: 33.43.61
331669	33.16.69
332120	33.21.20

Northern Chinese Cooking
(Shanxi)

The menu presented below is suitable for 4 people and would cost about
¥35 per person, not including drinks.

Chinese	Pinyin	English
冷 盘	Lěng pán	Assorted Cold Hors d'Oeuvres
香酥鸭	Xiāngsū yā	Fragrant Crisp Duck

炸大虾	Zhá dàxiā	Deep-Fried Prawns
龙须菜	Lóngxū cài	Asparagus
宫爆鸡丁	Gōngbào jīdīng	Diced Chicken Sautéed with Hot Pepper
杏仁豆腐	Xìngrén dòufu	Almond Beancurd
主 食	Shǔ shí	Cereal Dish (rice and noodles)

The Deep-Fried Prawns are highly favored at Beijing restaurants, and perhaps nowhere are they done better than at the Jin Yang. The giant prawns are heated in a pan with onion, ginger, garlic, and salted beans, stir-fried rapidly, and allowed to simmer until the sauce has almost dried. The prawns are then turned in molten lard a few times before serving.

The Diced Chicken Sautéed with Hot Pepper is another well-known dish, providing cubes of chicken slightly scorched on the outside but juicy and tender inside, served in a hot and spicy sauce.

HUAI YANG FAN ZHUANG

淮阳饭庄   Huai Yang Style Restaurant

西单北大街212号   212 Xi Dan Bei Dajie

电话： 660521   Telephone: 66.05.21

Eastern Chinese Cooking
(Jiangsu; Zhejiang)

This restaurant serves Yangtze food of the Huai Yang style. The name is derived from the Huai River and the city of Yangzhou, near Shanghai. The food tends to be very rich, and many of the dishes use seafood or fish and eels from the coastal waterways.

The menu presented below is suitable for 10 people and would cost about ¥40 per person, not including drinks.

Chinese	Pinyin	English
冷 盘	Lěng pán	Cold Hors d'Oeuvres
炮鳝鱼	Paò shànyú	Eel with Sesame Oil and Garlic
扒三白	Pā sānbái	Three Whites: Fish, Chicken, Bamboo Shoot Tips
香酥鸡	Xiāngsū jī	Crisp-Fragrant Chicken

Chinese	Pinyin	English
烧熏黄鱼	Shāo xūnhúangyú	Smoked Yellow Pike
炸虾排	Zhá xiā pái	Deep Fried Prawn Cutlets
爆炒鳝片	Bàochǎo shànpiàn	Sauteed Eel Slices
红油虾片	Hóng yóu xiāpiàn	Prawn Slices in Red Sauce
酽青椒	Ràng qîngjiāo	Stuffed Green Pepper
汤	Tāng	Soup

A specialty is Three Whites, otherwise known as Triple-White in Thick Wine Sauce, made by stir-frying chicken breast slices, then placing them over fish slices in the pan and frying them quickly on either side. Bamboo shoots, chicken broth, salt, ginger, wine sauce, and sugar are added to complete this dish.

KANG LE

康乐饭店	Health and Happiness Restaurant
安定门内大街259号	259 An Ding Men Nei Dajie
电话：443884	Telephone: 44.38.84

Southern Border Chinese Cooking
(Yunnan)

The menu presented below is suitable for 6 people and would cost about ¥35 per person, not including drinks.

Chinese	Pinyin	English
什锦拼盘	Shìjǐn pīnpán	Cold Hors d'Oeuvres
桃花饭	Táo huā fàn	Peach Flower Rice

Chinese	Pinyin	English
炸瓜枣冬笋	Zhágūazǎo dōngsǔn	Deep-Fried Winter Melon with Dates and Bamboo Shoots
汽锅油鸡	Qìguō yóujī	Steamed Chicken in Oil
香桃鸭方	Xiāngtáo yāfāng	Duck with Walnuts
鲜锅肉饼大虾	Dàxia xiāngūo ròubǐng	Pancake with Prawns
素烧四宝	Sùshāo sìbǎo	Four Vegetable Delicacies
过桥面	Guòqiáo miàn	Crossing-the-Bridge Noodles

The menu presented below is suitable for 6 people and would cost about ¥30 per person, not including drinks.

CHINESE	ENGLISH
四盖碗双拼	Four Cold Hors d'Oeuvres
桃花饭	Peach Flower Rice
炸瓜枣冬笋	Fried Winter Melon with Dates and Bamboo Shoots
香酥鸭	Fragrant Crispy Duck
清蒸活鱼	Steamed Fish with Ginger and Scallion
翡翠羹	Jade Spinach Soufflé
过桥面	Crossing-the-Bridge Noodles

Crossing-the-Bridge Noodles, so called because in the days of the Imperial Court the noodles are said to have been dropped into the pot of boiling water just as the chef reached the bridge to the Imperial City. By the time the pot arrived at the Emperor's table, the noodles were perfectly prepared for his immediate consumption. Kang Le's Jade Spinach Soufflé has a superb, velvety texture and is also appealing to the eye.

QING HAI

青海餐厅   Qing Hai Restaurant

东西北大街５５５号   Dong Si Bei Da Jie, 555

电话：４４２９４７   Telephone : 44.29.47

Northern and Qing Hai Regional Cooking

The menu presented below is suitable for 8 people and would cost about ￥40 per person, not including drinks.

Chinese	English
什锦拼盘	Assorted Cold Hors d'Oeuvres
鸡茸鱼翅	Sharksfin with Minced White Meat of Chicken
冬虫扒鸭	Stewed Duck in Winter Herbs
银千烤肉	Roast Pork with Silver Sprouts
芙蓉鸡片炸口柿	Chicken Puffs with Tomato Slices in Herbs
油泡肚仁焖珍	Stewed Tripe, Gizzard and Liver Platter in Wine and Soy Sauce
高力沃片茄合	Fried Eggplant with Kidney Slices
煎转活鱼	Sauteed Whole Fish in Ginger Sauce
干贝东瓜	Winter Melon Soup with Dried Scallops
醋椒三片	Three "Spicy and Sour" (pork, mushrooms, and bamboo shoots)
冰糖菠萝	Chilled Pineapple Slices

This restaurant is consistently good and is perhaps one of the most under-rated in Beijing.

Sharksfin with Minced White Meat of Chicken is a superb dish with chunks of sharksfin surmounted by an "island" of chicken meat. The combination of the two meats provides a succulent taste which will appeal to your palate.

Stewed Duck in Winter Herbs is a fragrant dish which gives off the fine aroma of herbs (mostly North China winter herbs). The duck is stuffed with the herbs and the flavor permeates the duck meat; the duck meat falls away from the bone during serving.

Other notable dishes on this menu are *Fried Eggplant with Kidney Slices*, (the flavors marry well together and the dish is visually appealing) and *Chicken Puffs with Tomato Slices in Herbs*.

同和居

西四南大街3号

电话：660925

Peace and Harmony Restaurant

3 Xi Si Nan Da Jie

Telephone: 66.09.25

Northern Chinese Cooking
(Shandong)

At this restaurant you may have an excellent meal for about ¥30 per head. However, if you wish to order a full banquet, the menu presented below is suitable for 5-6 people and would cost about ¥35 per person, not including drinks.

Chinese	Pinyin	English
冷 盘	Lěng pán	Cold Hors d'Oeuvres
扒鲍龙须菜	Pābaō lónghxū caì	Asparagus with Dried Abalone
蟹肉菜心	Xièròu cài xīn	Crab Meat with Vegetables
三不沾	Sān bù zhān	Three Non-Stick
香酥鸡	Xīang sū jī	Fragrant Crisp Chicken
四宝汤	Sì Bǎo tāng	Four Delicacies Soup
宫爆鸡丁	Gōngbào jīdīng	Diced Chicken with Chili and Peanuts
西法大虾	Xīfǎ dàxīa	Prawns Cooked Xifa Style
锅塌鱼	Gūotā yú	Dry-fried Fish
鸭肝冬笋	Yāgān dōngsǔn	Duck Liver with Bamboo Shoots

A specialty of the restaurant is Asparagus with Dried Abalone. Dried abalone is an expensive delicacy in China, and when combined with asparagus forms a dish with subtle flavor and contrasting textures.

Another well-known dish at this restaurant is the curiously named Three Non-Stick, or Triple None Stuck. It is an egg dish which derives its name from the fact that it sticks neither to the teeth, the spoon, nor the chopsticks.

The following menu is suitable for 7 people and would cost about ¥35 per person.

CHINESE	ENGLISH
什锦拼盘	Assorted Cold Hors d'Oeuvres
扒鲍龙须	Abalone with Asparagus Tips
三不拈	Three Non-Stick
香酥鸭	Fried Crispy Duck
虾干冬瓜	Winter Melon with Preserved Shrimp
宫保鸡丁	Sauteed Chicken Cubes with Chili and Peanuts
炸烹大虾	Deep-Fried Giant Prawns
炸笋鸡块	Crispy Chicken
芝麻鸭肝	Fried Duck Livers with Sesame Seeds
水果	Fresh Fruit

The *Abalone and Asparagus Tips* dish is prepared from dried, whole abalone, mixed with asparagus tips in a cream sauce. This dish, one of the finest on the restaurant's menu, has a delicate flavor and an interesting contrast in textures. *Fried Duck Livers with Sesame Seeds* are made with plump fried livers, rolled in sesame seeds. This dish has a pleasant, nutty flavor. The *Winter Melon with Preserved Shrimp* is different from the carved winter melon soup described elsewhere. This particular dish comprises chunks of winter melon served with preserved shrimps.

ZHEN JIANG

镇江饭庄	Zhen Jiang Restaurant
宣内大街	Xun Nei Da Jie
电话：662115，	Telephone: 66.21.15
662289	66.22.89

Eastern Chinese Cooking
(Jiangsu; Shanghai)

The menu presented below is suitable for 15 people and would cost about ¥35 per person, not including drinks.

Chinese	Pinyin	English
八个冷盘	Bāgè lěng pán	Eight Cold Hors d'Oeuvres
鸡蓉鱼翅	Jīróng yúchì	Chicken Puffs with Sharksfin
炸金钱大虾	Zhá jīnqián dàxîa	Golden Coin Prawns
羊肉串	Yángròu chuàn	Lamb Shashlik
龙须菜	Lóngzū caǐ	Asparagus
香果鸭	Xiānggǔo jī	Chicken in Fragrant Fruit
海杂拌	Hǎi Zábàn	Sea Food Mixture
红烧牛尾	Hóng shāo niúwěi	"Red Cook" Oxtail
口蘑鸭子	Kǒumó yāzi	Duck with Mushrooms
点 心	Diǎnxīn	Dessert
水 果	Shǔigǔo	Fresh Fruit

The restaurant specializes in food from Jiangsu Province and the Shanghai region. In these regions the "red cook" method of preparing food is well known.

In the menu above the dish featuring this technique is the "Red Cook" Oxtail. This is prepared by cooking an oxtail slowly in dark soy, ginger, wine, and brown sugar. The meat is cooked until it is ready to slide from the bone. The name of this process derives from the color given to the meats cooked in this way.

Another dish worthy of note is Golden Coin Prawns. The prawns are flattened and fried and when served have the appearance of golden coins.

You will note that as the origin of the cuisine moves further south, the dishes become more decorative and the names more descriptive.

Another specialty of the restaurant is Chicken Puffs with Sharks Fin which has been described under the "Feng Ze Yuan" Restaurant.

The Lamb Shaslik is excellent even though it is not a specialty of the region. It is well worth trying, particularly if you do not have an opportunity to visit one of the restaurants specializing in the preparation of Moslem food.

BEIJING KAO YA DIAN

北京烤鸭店   Peking Roast Duck Restaurant

王府井大街13号   13 Wang Fu Jing

电话：553310   Telephone: 55.33.10

Northern Chinese Cooking
(Beijing)

This restaurant is the best-known roast duck restaurant in Beijing. Because of its location near Beijing's major hospital it is called the "Sick Duck" by the locals.

The menu presented below is suitable for 8 people and would cost about ¥50 per person, not including drinks.

Chinese	Pinyin	English
冷 盘	Lěng pán	Cold Hors d'Oeuvres
炸鸭珍肝	Zhá yāzhen gā	Deep-Fried Duck Livers
宫爆鸭心	Gōngbào yāxīn	Duck Heart in Hot Garlic Sauce
西法大虾	Xīfǎ dàxīa	Prawns European Style
糟溜鸭三白	Zāoliǔ yā sānbái	Three Delicacies of Duck in Rice Wine
炒香菇笋片	Chǎo xiānggū sǔnpiàn	Fried Mushrooms and Bamboo Shoots
烤鸭	Kǎo yā	Roast Duck (Peking Style)
鸭骨菜汤	Yāgǔ cài tāng	Duck Bone Soup with Vegetables
拔丝山药	Bá sī shanyaò	Caramelized Yam
水 果	Shǔiguǒ	Fruits

The menu presented here is a classic Peking Duck menu, featuring dishes using all parts of the duck except the feathers. Even the webs of the feet are eaten.

Peking Roast Duck is one of Northern China's famous specialties. Prepared from a 3-to-4-month-old white Peking duck, the carcass is plugged, half filled with water, then roasted in the oven. Only wood of the ju-jube, pear tree, or apricot tree is used. While the outside of the duck is roasted and brought to a golden brown by basting, the inside of the bird is steamed by the evaporating water. The duck is roasted and steamed for about three quarters of an hour. When ready for serving, the whole duck is usually carried to the table on a platter, the chef often making an appearance to display his culinary creation. The duck is then returned to the kitchen, where the skin is cut in small squares. Then the pieces are served to the guests. The slices of golden skin are eaten by wrapping them inside thin crepes or in sesame rolls, dipped in a sauce of chopped leeks, cucumbers, and scallions. The *Duck Bone Soup* always follows the Peking Roast Duck dish. It has the appearance of a cream soup, but the texture of a consommé. Savor this soup slowly; it is a fine creation ending the duck portion of the banquet.

QIAN MEN KAO YA DIAN

前门烤鸭店   Qian Men Roast Duck Restaurant

前门大街32号   32 Qian Men Da Jie

电话：751379   Telephone: 75.13.79

Northern Chinese Cooking
(Beijing)

This restaurant is known as the "Big Duck" to distinguish it from the other branch known as the "Sick Duck." The food at the "Big Duck" is equally as good as that served in the "Sick Duck," although the restaurant lighting is far less subdued and the ambience probably less appealing.

The menu presented below is suitable for 8 people and would cost about ¥45 per person, not including drinks.

Chinese	Pinyin	English
冷盘	Lěng pán	Cold Hors d'Oeuvres
炸鸭肝	Zhá yāgān	Deep Fried Duck Liver
炒口蘑鸭心	Chǎo kǒumó yāixīn	Sautéed Mushroom and Duck Heart
干烧子鲍	Gānshāao zǐbāo	Sautéed Abalone in Garlic and Chili
烩四宝	Huì sìǎo	Assorted Four Delicacies from the Duck
鸭	Yā	Roast Duck
鸭骨汤	Yāgǔ tāng	Duck Bone Soup
拔丝萍果	Básī pínggǔo	Caramelized Apple
水果	Shǔigǔo	Fruit

HEPING KAO YA DIAN

和平烤鸭店

宣武和平门

电话：

("Super Duck"
or "McDonald Duck")

Xiañwu, Hepiñgmeñ

Telephone: 33.80.31

Northern Chinese Cooking
(Beijing)

"Heping Kao Ya Dan"—known to locals as the "Super Duck" because of its size, or the "Peaceful Duck" because of its location near the Peace Gate—serves the full complement of duck dishes and caters to a vast number of diners each day.

The following menu is suitable for 8 persons and would cost about ¥50 each, not including drinks.

Chinese	Pinyin	English
冷盘	Lěng pán	Cold Hors d'Oeuvres
宫爆鸭心	Gōngbào yāxīn	Duck Heart in Hot Garlic Sauce
干烧子鲍	Gānshāao zībāo	Sautéed Abalone in Garlic and Chili
糟溜鸭三白	Zāoliū yā sānbái	Three Delicacies of Duck in Rice Wine
炒香菇笋片	Chǎo xiānggū sǔnpiàn	Fried Mushrooms and Bamboo Shoots
烤鸭	Kǎo yā	Roast Duck (Peking Style)
鸭骨菜汤	Yāgǔ cài tāng	Duck Bone Soup with Vegetables
杏仁豆腐三果	Xìnrén dòufu sān gǔo	Almond Beancurd with Mixed Fruit

KAO ROU JI

烤肉季   Season for Roasting Meat Restaurant

前海东沿14号   14 Chienhai Dong Yen

电话：445921   Telephone: 44.59.21

Northern Chinese Cooking (Mongolian)

This restaurant is the only one in Beijing where you can dine on a balcony overlooking a lake, a refreshing experience in the hot summer months. You may also watch the meat being barbecued in a small kitchen just off the balcony. A delightful little restaurant, even though the menu is fairly restricted.

You may have a simple meal at this restaurant for as little as ¥25 per person, but if you wish to order a banquet the menu presented below is suitable for 4 people and would cost about ¥35 per person, not including drinks.

Chinese	Pinyin	English
冷盘	Lěng pán	Cold Hors d'Oeuvres
炸大虾	Zhá dàxiā	Deep-Fried Prawns

Chinese	Pinyin	English
桂花干贝	Guìhūa gānbèi	Cassia-Dried Scallops with Eggs
鲍鱼龙须	Baōyú lóngxū	Abalone with Asparagus
烤　肉	Kǎoròu	Barbecued Lamb (Mongolian Style)
鸡　蛋	Jīdàn	Eggs

The specialty is obviously the Barbecued Beef or Lamb; it is served in a bowl to each guest and you should add some of the sauces provided. Sesame buns are usually eaten with this course.

The Deep-Fried Prawns are also well prepared at Kou Rou Ji and are definitely worth ordering.

Menus from the Best Beijing Restaurants

We present here the complete menus from two of the top restaurants in Beijing: Feng Ze Yuan and Sichuan.

The menus are provided in Chinese with English translations. The Pinyin form is also provided for those who may wish to practise and improve their Chinese. You should consult the supplement dealing with the Chinese language to familiarize yourself with the tones and the system of phonetics adopted.

The complete menus should prove of value for visitors who know how to put together a variety of dishes for a banquet or for those who wish to select a few dishes without ordering a full banquet. However, when in doubt, leave yourself in the hands of the restaurant chefs, who will select dishes for you; or consult recommended banquet manus.

FENG ZE YUAN RESTAURANT

丰泽园 — Garden of Abundance and Colour

珠市口西大街 183 号 — 183 Zhu Shi Kou Street (West), Peking

电话：332828 — Telephone: 33.28.28

Many Chinese believe this restaurant (pronounced "Foong Tze Yan") to be the finest in Beijing, and it therefore ranks as one of the most distinguished Chinese restaurants in the world. As in almost all restaurants in Beijing, the decor is simple and unpretentious; the food alone assures fame.

If you enjoy food, you cannot afford to miss the experience of dining here; to host a banquet here is to pay your guests the highest compliment. If you select rare dishes you will pay a goodly sum, but you can also dine well and inexpensively if you choose with care.

You may prefer to let the restaurant decide on the dishes after advising them of what you want to pay per person and the total number of guests attending. You can expect to pay a minimum of ¥50 per person, not including drinks, for a reasonable banquet, but add ¥25-40 or more per person if you wish to include rare and special dishes.

Chinese	Pinyin	English
	Lěng cài léi	Cold Dishes
拌鸭掌	Bàn yazhǎng	Marinated Duck Web
三丝冬粉	Sānsī dōngfěn	Three Shreds with Winter Noodles
干贝松翠丝	Gānbèi sōngcuìst	Scallop Shreds with Scallion
蜜汁火腿	Mì zhì huǒtuǐ	Ham in Honey
糟鸭片	Zāo yāpiàn	Duck Slices in Wine
白片鸡	Bái piàn jī	Chicken Slices
卤珍肝	Lǔ zhēn gān	Liver and Gizzard Stew
糟白肉	Zāo báiròu	Cold Pork Slices Marinated in Wine Essence
鸡丝黄瓜	Jīsī huángguā	Chicken Shreds with Cucumber Shreds
辣黄瓜条	Là huángguā tiáor	Cucumber Slices with Chili
海味类	Hǎiwèi lèi	Seafood
清汤燕窝	Qīngtāng yànwō	Clear Soup with Bird's Nest
芙蓉燕窝	Fúróng yànwō	Egg Velvet with Bird's Nest
砂锅炖鱼翅	Shāguō dùn yúchì	Sharksfin Stewed in Unglazed Pot
红扒鱼翅	Hóng pá yúchì	Grilled Sharksfin
桂花鱼翅	Guìhuā Yúchì	Sharksfin with Cassia and Flower Eggs
干烤鱼翅	Gān kǎo yúchì	Dry Stewed Sharksfin
红烧三丝鱼翅	Hóng shāo sānsī yúchì	Stewed Sharksfin with Three Shreds in Brown Sauce

Chinese	Pinyin	English
鸡蓉鱼翅	Jīróng yúchì	Sharksfin with Chicken Puffs
红扒鱼唇	Hóng pá yúchún	Red Grilled Fish Lips
白扒鱼肚	Bái pá yúdǔ	White Grilled Fish Tripe
鸡蓉鱼肚	Jīróng yúdǔ	Fish Tripe with Chicken Puffs
红烧海参	Hóng shāo hǎishēn	Sea Cucumber in Brown Sauce
汆鸡茸五丝	Cuān jīróng wǔsī	Chicken Velvet with Five Shreds
汆四宝	Cuān sìbǎo	Four Delicacies
鸡茸干贝菜花	Jīróng gānbèi càihuā	Scallop with Cauliflower and Chicken Velvet
红烧元鱼	Hóng shāo yuán yú	Stewed Fish in Brown Sauce
糖醋鱼片	Táng cù yūpiàn	Fish Slices in Sweet and Sour Sauce
砂锅鱼唇	Shāguō yúchún	Fish Lips in Unglazed Casserole
葱烧海参	Cōng shāo hǎishēn	Sea Cucumber with Scallions
山东海参	Shāndōng hǎishēn	Shandong Sea Cucumber
胡辣海参	Húlà hǎishēn	Sea Cucumber with Pepper
清汤八珍	Qīngtāng bāzhēn	Soup with Eight Delicacies
清汤杂拌	Qīngtāng zábàr	Clear Soup
鸡油四宝	Jīyóu sìbǎo	Four Delicacies in Chicken Oil
扒龙须鲍鱼	Pá lóngzū bàoyú	Grilled Abalone with Asparagus
扒鱼肚菜心	Pá yúdǔ càixīn	Grilled Fish Tripe with Tender Vegetables
扒龙须菜心	Pá lóngzū càixīn	Grilled Asparagus with Hearts of Green

Chinese	Pinyin	English
扒三白	Pá sānbái	Grilled Three Whites
扒裙边	Pá qúnbiān	Grilled "Shirt Edge" (Turtle)
清蒸元鱼	Qīng zhēng yuányú	Steamed Fish
芙蓉鱼片	Fúróng yúpiàn	Eggwhite Puffs with Fish Slices
五柳鱼	Wǔliǔ yú	Five Willow Fish
赛螃蟹	Sài pángziè	Crab Contest
干烧活鱼	Gān shāo huó yú	Fresh Fish in Soy and Chili Sauce
醋椒活鱼	Cù jiāo huó yú	Fresh Fish in Chili and Vinegar
清蒸活鱼	Qīng zhēng huó yù	Steamed Fresh Fish
糖醋活鱼	Táng cù huó yú	Fresh Fish with Sour and Sweet Flavor
酱汁活鱼	Jiàng zhī huó yú	Fried Fish in Soy Sauce and Wine
酱糟鱼	Jiā zāo yú	Fried Fish
鱼锅	Yúguō	Fish in Casserole
红烧鱼	Hóng shūo yú	Fish in Brown Sauce
扒熊掌	Pá xióng zhǎng	Grilled Bear's Paw
炸鱼条	Shá yútiáo	Deep-Fried Fish Slices
雪花鱼片	Xuěhuá yúpiàn	Snowy Fish Slices
芫爆鳝鱼片	Yán bào shàn yúpiàn	Stir Fried Eel Slices
爆炒鳝鱼丝	Bàp chǎo shànyúsī	Stir Fried Eel Shreds
油焖大虾	Yóu men dàxiā	Prawn Stewed in Oil
炸烹大虾	Zhá pēng dàxiā	Deep-Fried Prawn

Chinese	Pinyin	English
雪花大虾	Xuěhuá dàxiā	Snowy Prawn
蕃茄大虾	Fānqié dàxiā	Prawn with Tomato
软炸大虾	Ruǎn zhá dàxiā	Soft Fried Prawn
炸虾托	Zhá xiātuō	Deep-Fried Prawn Canape
青炒虾仁	Qīng chǎo xiārén	Stir-Fried Shrimps
炸虾球	Zhá xiāgiú	Deep-Fried Prawn Meat Balls
桂花干贝	Guìhuā gānbèi	Cassia Scallop
炒芙蓉干贝	Chǎo fúróng gābèi	Fried Scallop with Egg-white
会乌龟蛋	Huì wūyú dàn	Stewed Turtle Eggs
扒鲍鱼菜心	Pá bàoyú càixīn	Grilled Abalone and Vegetable
油爆鱼肝丁	Yóu ba.go yú gāndīng	Oil Fried Fish Liver Slices
象眼鸽蛋	Xiàng yǎn gēdàn	"Elephant Eye" Pigeon Egg
锅塌鲍鱼盒	Guō baòyú hé	Abalone Cake
糟溜三白	Zāo liū sānbái	Three Whites in Wine Essence
山东菜	Shāndōng cài	Shandong Vegetable
什锦丝冬粉	Shíjǐnsī dōng fén	Assorted Shreds with Vermicelli
氽鱼腐丸子	Cuān yú fǔ wánzi	Fish and Beancurd Balls in Soup
醋椒三片	Cù jiāo sān piàn	Three Kinds of Slices in Vinegar and Chili
三鲜汤	Sān xiān tāng	Three Delicacies Soup
氽鱼片黄瓜	Cuān yúpiàn huángguā	Fish Slices with Cucumber
氽鱼卷	Cuān yú juǎn	Fish Rolls in Soup

Chinese	Pinyin	English
鸡鸭肉类	<u>Jī vā ròulèi</u>	<u>Chicken and Duck</u>
酒蒸肥鸭	Jiǔ zhēng féiyā	Duck Steamed with Wine
香酥肥鸭	Ziāng sū féiyā	Fragrant Crisp Duck
干烤肥鸭	Gān káo féiyā	Dry Stewed Duck
香酥鸡	Ziāngsū jī	Fragrant Crisp Chicken
酒蒸鸡	Jiǔ hēng jī	Chicken Steamed with Wine
山东烧鸡	Shǎndōng shāojī	Shandong Roast Chicken
酱爆鸡丁	Jiàngbào jīdīng	Chicken Slices in Brown Sauce
芙蓉鸡片	Fúróng jīpiàn	Chicken Slices with Egg-white Puffs
扒鸡腿	Pá jītuǐ	Grilled Chicken Leg
香酥鸡腿	Ziāng sū jī tuǐ	Crisp Fragrant Chicken Leg
目鱼炖鸡	Mùyú dùn jī	Stewed Chicken with Plaice
糟烩鸭四宝	Zāo huì yā sìbǎo	Four Duck Delicacies
糟蒸鸭肝	Zāo zhēng yāgān	Steamed Duck Liver in Wine
清炸蒸肝	Qīng zhá zhēn gān	Deep-Fried Gizzard and Liver
炸芝麻鸭肝	Zhá zhīma yāgān	Deep-Fried Duck Liver (Sesame-Coated)
面包鸭肝	Miamgba.mo yāgān	Bread and Duck Liver
炸五丝筒	Zhá wǔsītǒng	Deep-Fried Five Shreds Rolls
火锅	Huǒguō	Hot Pot
芫爆里肌	Yán bào lǐjí	Sauteed Pork Fillet
芫爆肚片	Yán bào dǔpiàn	Saufeed Chicken Tripe

Chinese	Pinyin	English
油爆双脆	Yóu ba.go shuāngcuì	Oil-Fried Double Crisps
辣子鸡丁	Làzi jīdīng	Chicken Slices with Chili
软炸鸡	Ruǎn zhá jī	Soft-Fried Chicken
炸笋鸡块	Zhá sǔn jī kuài	Deep-Fried Tender Chicken Slices
炒生鸡丝蜇皮	Chǎo shēng jīsī zhépí	Sautéed Chicken Shreds and Jellyfish
烩鸡丁鲜蘑	Huì yādīng Ziānmó	Diced Duck with Mushrooms
鸡蓉菜心	Jīróng càixīu	Chicken Velvet with Hearts of Green Vegetable
冬笋焖胗	Dōngsǔn mèn zhēn	Bamboo Shoots Stewed with Gizzard
香菇焖胗	Ziānggu mèn zhēn	Mushrooms Stewed with Gizzard
烩里肌丝	Huì lìjísī	Stewed Pork Filet Shreds
酱爆里肌丁	Jiàng baò lǐjídīng	Diced Pork Fillet in Brown Sauce
清炸里肌	Qīng zhá lǐjí	Deep-Fried Pork Filet
锅贴香菇盒	Gūotiē xiānggū hé	Pan Fried Mushroom Cake
蔬菜类	<u>Sù cài lei</u>	<u>Vegetables</u>
香菇菜花	Xiānggū càihuā	Mushrooms with Cauliflower
锅贴豆腐	Guōtiē dòufu	Beancurd Dumplings
烩鲜蘑碗豆	Huì xiānmó wāndòu	Fresh Mushroom with Lima Beans
口蘑焖扁豆	Kǒumó mèn biǎndòu	Mushrooms with Snow Peas
汆银耳	Cuān yíněr	Snow Mushroom Soup

Chinese	Pinyin	English
糟煨冬笋	Zāo wēi dōngsǔn	Bambooshoots Marinated in Wine Essence
甜菜类	<u>Tián cài lèi</u>	<u>Desserts</u>
冰糖莲子	Bīngtang liánzi	Crystalized Sugar with Lotus Seeds
拔丝莲子	Bāsī liánzi	Toffee Lotus Seeds
八宝莲子饭	Bābǎo liánzifàn	Eight Treasure Glutinous Rice with Lotus Seeds
拔丝萍果	Básī píngguǒ	Toffee Apples
拔丝山药	Básī shān yào	Toffee Yam
炒三不沾	Chǎo sān bu zhān	Sautéed Three Nonstick
杏仁豆腐菠罗	Zìngrén dòufu bōluó	Almond Beancurd with Pineapple
冰镇三果	Bīngzhèn sānguǒ	Three Iced Fruits and Nuts
炒三泥	Chǎo sān ní	Stir-Fried Three Mashed Things
面点类	Miàn diǎn léi	Noodles, Rice

SICHUAN RESTAURANT

四川饭店

Sichuan Restaurant
(formerly "Cheng Du")

西绒线胡同51号

51 West Rong Xian Lane, Peking

电话：336356

Telephone: 33.63.56

　The Sichuan Restaurant (pronounced "sss-chewarn") vies with the Fang Shan and the Ze Yuan as the most prestigious restaurant in all of Beijing. It certainly has one of the best settings of any restaurant in the capital, with its fine courtyards and contrasting red and gold decor, befitting the style and opulence of its (reputed) former owner, Yuan Shihkai, the general who tried unsuccessfully to become emperor in the earlier years of the century.

　The name of the restaurant stems from the well-known central province. The former name, Cheng Du, is the capital of that province. The area is famous throughout China for its hot and spicy food, but, in keeping with Chinese gastronomy, there is always in a banquet menu a fine balance of different foods providing both contrast and interest to the palate.

You can expect to pay a minimum of ¥40 per person, not including drinks, or a reasonable banquet. The inclusion of rare and special dishes could add ¥25-40 per head or more to the bill.

The restaurant's entire menu is presented below.

Chinese	Pinyin	English
冷　菜	Lěng cài	Cold Dishes
怪味鸡	Guài weìr jī	Chicken in Peanut and Pepper Sauce
麻辣牛肉	Má là nuí roù	Beef with Pepper and Chili
姜汁菠菜	Jiāng zhī bó cài	Spinach in Ginger Juice
宜宾糟蛋	Yí bīn zāo dàn	Yibin Preserved Wine Eggs
陈皮牛肉	Chénpí nuí roù	Beef with Orange Peel
椒麻鸭掌	Jiāo má yā zhǎng	Duck Foot Web with Pepper and Chili
红油牛肋	Hóng yóu núi juī	Beef Tendon in Red Pepper Oil
烟熏酥鱼	Yā xūn sūyú	Smoked Crisp Fish
热菜	Re cài	Hot Dishes
红烧熊掌	Hóng shāo xúng zhǎng	Bear's Paw in Brown Sauce
包烧鱼翅	Bāo shāo yú chì	Sharksfin in Brown Sauce
三丝鱼翅	Sān sī yú chì	Sharksfin with Three Shreds
三鲜鲍鱼	Sān xiān bāo yú	Abalone with Three Shreds
黄焖干鲍	Huǎng mēn gān bāo	Stewed Abalone
家常海参	Jīa cháng hǎi shēn	Peppery Sea Cucumber
锅巴海参	Guō bā hǎi shēn	Crisp Rice with Sea Cucumber
干烧青鱼	Gān shāo qīng yú	Fish in Hot Sauce
豆瓣桂鱼	Doù bàn guài yú	Fish in Black Bean Sauce

Chinese	Pinyin	English
豆腐鲤鱼	Dòu fu lǐ yú	Carp with Bean Curd
清蒸时鱼	Qīng zhāng shí yú	Steamed Fresh Fish in Season
干烧大虾	Gān shāo dà xiā	Prawn in Sichuan Sauce
鱼香大虾	Yū xiāng dà xiā	Prawn with Garlic and Chili
黄焖大虾	Huáng mēn dà xiā	Stewed Prawns
网油虾卷	Wǎng yóu xiā juǎnr	Prawn Rolls in Oil
樟茶鸭子	Zhāng chá yāzi	Duck Smoked with Camphor and Tea Leaves
豆渣鸭腩	Doù zhā yā fǔ	Duck Breasts with Bean Curd
黄酒煨鸡	Huáng jiǔ wēi yā	Duck Stewed with Rice Wine
大酿鸭腩	Dà rāng yā fǔ	Stuffed Duck Breasts in Wine
米熏子鸡	Mǐ xūn zǐjī	Smoked Tender Chicken
网油灯笼鸡	Wǎng yóu dēng lóng jī	Lantern Chicken with Oil
胡辣鸡丁	Hú là jīdīng	Chicken Slices with Pepper and Chili
姜汁子鸡	Jiang zhī zǐ jī	Tender Chicken with Ginger Juice
鱼香肉丝	Yú xiāng roù sī	Pork Shreds with Fishy Flavor
水煮牛肉	Shǔi zhǔ núi roù	Stewed Beef
干扁牛肉丝	Gā biǎn núi roù sī	Beef Shreds Sichuan Style
米粉蒸肉	Mǐ fěn zhēng roù	Steamed Pork with Rice Flour
回锅肉	Húi gūo roù	Twice-Cooked Pork Slices
小笼牛肉	Xīao lóng núi roù	Beef in Small Bamboo Steamer

Chinese	Pinyin	English
大让竹笋	Dà rāng zhú xùn	Bamboo Sprouts
鲜蘑兰笋	Xiān mó lán sǔn	Fresh Mushrooms and Bamboo Shoots
鱼香茄子	Yúxiāng qié zi	Eggplant with Fishy Flavor
摇蛀时菜	Yáo zhù shí cài	Fresh Vegetables with Dried Scallops
鸡油季豆	Jī yóu jì dòu	Green Beans in Chicken Oil
麻辣豆腐	Má là doùfu	Beancurd with Pepper and Chili
熊掌豆腐	Xúng Zhǎng doùfu	Bear's Paw with Beancurd
汤	<u>Tāng</u>	<u>Soup</u>
清汤燕菜	Qīng tāng yàn cài	Clear Soup with Vegetables
竹荪兰笋汤	Zhú xùn lán sǔn tāng	Bamboo Sprouts and Bamboo Shoots Soup
清汤干糕	Qīng tāng gān gāo	Clear Soup with Dried Cakes
酸菜尤鱼汤	Suān cài yóu yú tāng	Pickled Vegetables with Squid Soup
清蒸杂烩	Qīng zhēng zá huì	Hodgepodge Soup
开水白菜	Kāi shǔi bái cài	Boiled Water with Cabbage
口蘑豆花	Kǒu mó doù hūa	Soft Bean Curd with Mushrooms
原汤素烩	Yuán tāng cù huì	Consommé
甜菜	<u>Tián cài</u>	<u>Desserts</u>
炒核桃泥	Chǎo hé táoní	Stir-Fried Mashed Walnut
雪花桃泥	Xǔe hūa táoní	Snowy Mashed Walnut
菠罗凉醪糟	Bōlúo liáng niào zāo	Cold Pineapple in Wine Essence
醪糟百子果羹	Niào zāo bǎi zǐ gǔo gēng	Fruit in Rice Wine

Chinese	Pinyin	English
冰汁凉桃脯	Bīng zhī liáng táo fǔ	Iced Peach Slices
冰糖银耳	Bīng táng yíngěr	Crystalized Sugar with Snow Mushrooms
小吃	<u>Xiǎo chī</u>	<u>Snacks</u>
牛肉焦饼	Niúròu jiāo bǐng	Pancake with Beef
玻璃烧卖	Bōli shāomài	Glassy Shaomai (Dumplings with Meat Fillings)
担担面	Dān dan miàn	Dan Dan Noodles (Hot Sauce)
红油水饺	Hóng yóu shǔi jiǎo	Dumplings with Chili Oil
珍珠麻元	Zhēn zhu má yuán	Pearl Balls of Glutinous Rice
四川汤元	Sìchuān tāng yuán	Sichuan Glutinous Rice Balls
燕窝粑	Yànwō ba	Swallow's Nest Cake
鸡丝凉面	Jīsī liáng miàn	Cold Noodles with Chicken Shreds
罗卜丝饼	Lúobo sī bǐng	Cake with Vegetable Shreds

so na
(Clarinet)

GUANGZHOU (CANTON)

Center of Foreign Trade

Guangzhou, capital of the province of Guangdong, is a pleasant city of tropical parks and long streets flanked by cool, shady arcades. It is an important industrial center and its port, Whampoa, is South China's major foreign trade port.

In the early days of this century Guangzhou, like Shanghai, had a notorious reputation. Most of the city comprised a vast sprawl of makeshift shacks threaded by tiny lanes and serviced by open sewers. The poor—and they were the greater part of the population—lived in dreadful hovels, surrounded by putrid canals. Malnutrition and disease were widespread.

A modernization campaign got under way in the 1920's and large sections of the town were pulled down; in about 18 months almost 25 miles of streets, pavements and sewers were put down. The layout of the existing city largely reflects the major work program undertaken during this period, although there have been considerable improvements in public amenities since the Communists came to power in 1949.

The city is located on a bend of the Pearl River with the major portion lying to the north. It is bisected to form an eastern and western sector by the broad Liberation Avenue, or Jiefang Li; it is also bisected by an east-west road called Sun Yatsen Avenue, or Zhong Shan Lu.

The inhabitants thus find it convenient to describe the location of places in Guangzhou by sector. Most of the main streets run gently downhill from north to south and end at the river's edge. This serves as a useful directional aid when you are wandering in the city. However, not all the streets end at the river's edge.

The history of the city has long been associated with trade routes which pass through the province, making it a center for foreign commerce for over 2,000 years. Although the origins of the town are not clearly known, the first settlement is believed to have been established in the third century B.C. It is recorded that merchants from Rome visited the town during the Han Dynasty (B.C.206–A.D.220). Historical records also show that a large Moslem colony existed as early as the seventh century A.D.; a mosque had been established and contacts with the Middle East had developed. Centuries later recognition of the settlement's growing trading importance was given (in A.D.714) when one of the Tang Emperors established officials there to oversee foreign trade, in effect formally establishing the first official trading port in China.

In the tenth century the city was recognized as the capital of the autonomous dynasty of the Southern Han when it was known as Xing Wang Su. In those days the city maintained and developed contacts with Persian, Hindu, and Arab traders.

The first European influence dates from 1514 when the Portuguese Embassy arrived. Sea links with China were important, for the "Silk Road" across Asia was no longer a safe caravan route. In 1557 the Portuguese obtained permission from the Ming to settle on an island which they called Macao, some 70 miles downstream from Guangzhou. Then came the Spanish and the Dutch. The next to appear in the China Seas were the British, but they did not establish themselves to any great extent until the early eighteenth century, preferring to concentrate their efforts in India.

By 1715 the British East India Company had become the most important firm trading with China, but like other companies it was severely limited by the "Eight Regulations" which imposed strict sanctions on the conduct of all trade and restricted the movement of merchants. To keep foreigners out, one Chinese regulation stipulated that vessels could anchor only at Whampoa, some 13 miles below the town center, to load and unload. By the early nineteenth century England had emerged as the most powerful nation in the western world, and to underpin its growing influence in the Far East the British government "offered" a treaty regulating trade with China, an offer that was not considered acceptable by the Chinese court. The differences between the British government and the Chinese court set the scene for the conflict that was to break out.

By this time British trade with China involved the exchange of various English products for Chinese tea and silk. The balance of trade in China's favor was made up by payments of silver by the English. From 1800 onwards opium from India was offered as a substitute for silver, the original owners of the opium being the British East India Company, although it was sold to China by another organization. As opium imports into China were forbidden, it had to be smuggled in.

Eventually the illicit traffic increased to such an extent that its value equaled that of legitimate imports into China.

The conflict between the Chinese authorities who attempted to put down the illicit trade, the Chinese and British merchants who were profiting handsomely from the business, and the government of Britain which was trying to force concessions from the Chinese government in an effort to open up trade even further, led eventually to the Opium Wars, which began in 1839. At the conclusion of the Second Opium War of the mid-1850s, foreign merchants who had returned to find their warehouses and factories burned decided, with the backing of their governments, to establish a foreign enclave. An island was created from a partially submerged sandbank in the Pearl River in the heart of Guangzhou, and by 1861 over 40 acres of land had been released for this purpose. Thus from the 1860s to 1949, with a short wartime intermission in 1941–46, foreign domination of Guangzhou came from Sha Mian.

Along with western intrusion came revolutionary ideas, and by the early 1900s Guangzhou was a center of revolutionary activity. The sparks of the new ideas were fanned by widespread Chinese resentment of the power and influence possessed by foreigners operating in China. These new ideas eventually led to the overthrow of the Qing Dynasty by the revolutionary forces of Sun Yatsen in 1911. Much later, Mao Zedong and other leading Communists furthered the revolutionary reputation of Guangzhou by establishing the National Peasant Movement there during 1925 and 1926. Dedicated revolutionaries were trained to spread the Communist ideology throughout China.

Guangzhou was occupied by the Japanese at the end of 1938 during the Sino-Japanese war, and the city was once again under foreign control until the Japanese army withdrew at the conclusion of World War II. In the ensuing war between the Communists and the Nationalists, Guangzhou remained in the hands of the Nationalists until October 1949, when Communist armies took the city.

EXPLORING GUANGZHOU

Guangzhou Trade Fair

The Chinese Export Commodities Fair, or Guangzhou Trade Fair, is held twice a year, from 15 April-15 May and 15 October-15 November at the Guangzhou Foreign Trade Center. China conducts a great deal of its foreign trade—now estimated at about 15 percent of the total—at the Fair. Each Fair is attended by more than 25,000 businessmen.

The Fairground is located between the Guangzhou railway station and the Dong Fang Hotel. Many of China's vast range of products and commodities are on display, and over 40,000 different items are available for sale.

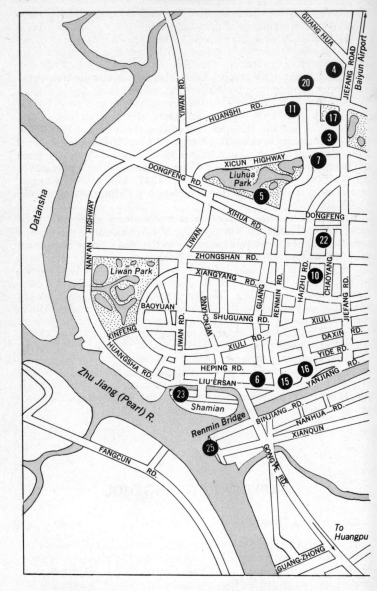

Points of Interest

1) Antique Shop
2) Bai Yun Hotel and Friendship Store
3) Guangzhou Foreign Trade Center
4) Cenotaph to the Anti-British Struggle at Sanyuanli
5) Children's Palace
6) Cultural Park
7) Dongfang Hotel
8) Guangdong Provincial Museum and Luxun Museum
9) Guangzhou Hotel
10) Huaisheng Mosque
11) Liuhua Guesthouse
12) Mausoleum of the Seventy-Two Martyrs
13) Memorial Park for the Martyrs of Guangzhou Uprising
14) Memorial Hall to Dr. Sun Yat Sen

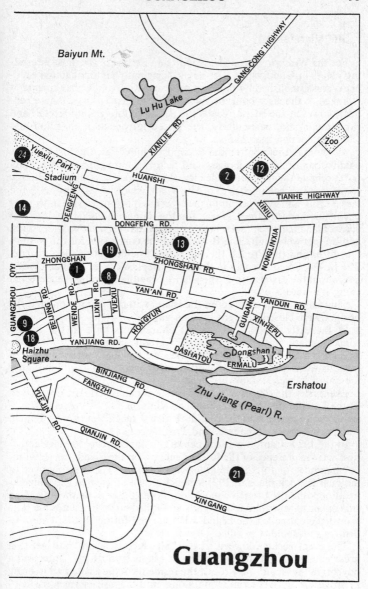

Baiyun Mt.

Lu Hu Lake

GANG-CONG HIGHWAY

Zoo

24 Yuexiu Park
Stadium

XIANLIE RD.

HUANSHI

2   12

TIANHE HIGHWAY

14

DENGFENG

DONGFENG RD.

XINIU

19

13

ZHONGSHAN

1

ZHONGSHAN RD.

NONGLINXIA

8

YAN'AN RD.

BEIJING RD.

WENDE RD.

LIXIN RD.

YUEXIU

HONGYUN

YANDUN RD.

GUGANG

XINHEPU

GUANGZHOU QIYI

9

18

YANJIANG RD.

DASHATOU

Dongshan

ERMALU

Haizhu
Square

BINJIANG RD.

FANGZHI

Zhu Jiang (Pearl) R.

Ershatou

YUEJIN RD.

QIANJIN RD.

21

XIN GANG

Guangzhou

15) Nanfang Department Store
16) Roman Catholic Cathedral
17) Orchid Garden
18) Overseas Chinese Hotel
19) Peasant Movement Institute and
    Exhibition Hall of the Revolution
20) Railroad Station
21) Sun-Yat-Sen University
22) Temple of the Six Banyan Trees and
    Liurong Pagoda

23) Zhenhai Tower
24) Zhoutouju Pier (to Hong
    Kong/Macau)
25) White Swan Hotel

Sha Mian Island

For the Western visitor Sha Mian Island is one of the most interesting places in Guangzhou. The island, originally an uninhabited sandbank, was established by building retaining walls and embankments; it is linked to the river bank by two small bridges. To the Chinese resident, however, the island recalls the period of foreign interference and exploitation and, particularly, the forced introduction of opium into China by foreign merchants.

In the mid-1850s, after the Second Opium War, the foreign merchants found their warehouses and factories burned and, rather than try to rebuild them again in the city, they decided to establish a foreign enclave on the reclaimed area of Sha Mian, which literally means "sand face." This aim was accomplished with a portion of the indemnity payments made by the Chinese for the damage caused. By 1861, 44 acres of land had been reclaimed, and embankments, paths, wide roads, and bridges were built. The British had the concession for the western four-fifths and the French the remaining one-fifth at the eastern end. The British Consulate was in the main street, while the French Consulate was at the eastern tip of the island. Magnificent villas were erected along the water's edge.

Chinese were not allowed on the island without permission, and the bridges were closed at night by iron gates.

In the early 1860s a Protestant church was built in the British concession and in the 1880s a small Catholic church was built in the French concession. The broad avenues were planted with a variety of trees, gardens were laid out, and tennis courts, a sailing club, and a football field were established.

Eventually the offices of several western banks were set up, as well as the hotel of distinction called The Victoria. By 1911 over 300 foreigners were resident on the island: British, French, Americans, Dutch, Italians, Germans, Japanese, and Portuguese.

In the 1920s Canton was the center of Chinese revolutionary activities, and the presence of the foreign enclave on the island was a continual reminder of foreign domination of China. The first boilover of indignation took place in 1925 when a crowd massed on the embankment opposite the French concession. Foreign troops on the Sha Mian side opened fire with machine guns and killed 60 or 70 Cantonese. The crowd then attacked the island and incurred further losses. One resident of the island was killed.

The event became known as the "Sha Kee Incident" and led to a great number of anti-foreign demonstrations throughout China and a boycott of the island. As a result the residents of the island had to bring in provisions upriver from Hong Kong until the restrictions were finally lifted.

Life quieted down on the island after the turbulent early '20s, and even when the Japanese took Canton at the end of 1938 there were few changes, although some residents left for Hong Kong. However, when Pearl Harbor was attacked in 1941, the foreign residents of Sha Mian were interned by the Japanese at Shanghai. After the war many residents went back to the island under the assumption that business would return to normal. But by October 1949 the Communist forces were in control, and by December 1950 all foreign assets were frozen and the few remaining foreigners left Sha Mian for good.

When you visit the island you can see the grand old buildings. Now they have a tired and worn look about them; the paint is peeling, pieces of masonry are falling out of the walls, the gardens are unkempt. The French Catholic church on Central Avenue is now a printing factory, and Christ Church has been converted into office buildings.

You will enjoy strolling along Central Avenue looking at these relics of the colonial past. Be sure you make a detour to the riverside embankment, where you can walk under the shade of the huge banyan trees, watch the multitude of river craft, or simply observe the Chinese schoolchildren practicing their sports and learning gymnastics.

Peasant Movement Institute

The Institute is housed in what was once a temple of Confucius and is located north of Sun Yatsen Street.

The exterior of the temple is in excellent condition, and you should take care to note the beautiful roof and the fine examples of glazed ceramic animals on the roof lines. The temple dates from the Ming and was originally constructed in the sixteenth century. In 1923 the Third Congress of the Chinese Congress Party decided to found the Peasant Movement Institute, and the temple building was chosen as the site for this new institution.

Students, drawn mainly from the peasant class, were trained to spread the Communist doctrine and, on completion of their studies, went out into the provinces of China to lead the movement. Mao Zedong was in charge of the Institute from March 1926, and he worked alongside Zhou Enlai and other Communist revolutionaries who became well known during and after the revolution. The staff and students of the school dispersed in 1927 when the Canton Commune was crushed by the Guomindang (or KMT).

The Institute has been restored, and you will see Mao's office and bedroom, dormitories of the students, the dining hall, the lecture rooms, and the wash rooms, complete with students' towels, mugs, and toothbrushes.

Exhibition Hall of the Revolution

The Exhibition Hall is located alongside the Peasant Movement Institute in a modern building completed in 1960. It houses a collection of interesting historical photographs and texts concerning the revolution, particularly those relating to Mao Zedong and Zhou Enlai and other famous revolutionary leaders. There is also a fine model of the boat used by the delegates at the first meeting of the Communist Party at Shanghai in 1921 when they had to flee from the city to escape the police.

Temple of the Six Banyan Trees

The temple is located in Liu Rong Jie, or Six Banyan Trees Street. It is not too far from the mosque. The Temple of the Six Banyan Trees is famous for the pagoda (called the Hua Ta or Lui Rong Pagoda), which stands beside it and is one of the most familiar landmarks in Guangzhou.

The temple is believed to have been founded in A.D.479 and the original pagoda in A.D.537. The pagoda was burned down in 1098, but a year later the famous poet Su Dong Po visited the temple and admired the six banyan trees. His reference to them in a poem well known in China has given the temple its name.

If you cannot get access to the grounds, the best view of the pagoda is from the minaret of the Mosque. The pagoda is decorated; it is 9 stories high, built on an octagonal base, and 180 feet high.

The Huaisheng Mosque

The Huaisheng Mosque is located in Guang Ta Lu Street south of Zhong Shan Lu, and is reputed to be the longest-established mosque in China.

Iron gates bar the entrance, but inside the archway high up on the right-hand side is a button which the visitor should press to gain entry. You will be ushered through a small pavilion into a courtyard surrounded by white walls and enclosing a number of shade trees. On the far side is the Prayer Room with modern Arabic script on the walls. Towering over the site is the 120-foot-high minaret. The original mosque is said to have been established in A.D.627 by an uncle of Mohammed, but the present buildings are of recent construction and have little architectural interest.

The minaret is a gray cement-rendered building with an inner staircase leading up to the traditional balcony near the top; there are 153 steps. From the balcony there is an excellent view of some of the major sites of Guangzhou: to the north is the Pagoda of the Six Banyan Trees; beyond the pagoda is the concrete tower of the Yue Xiu, and beyond, the radio tower on the hill in the Yue Xiu Park; just below the radio tower you will note a blue-tiled roof which belongs to the Sun Yatsen monument (actually a theater capable of seating over 5,000 people); to the right of that in the northeast is the 33-story Bai Yun Hotel.

If you walk around the balcony and look to the south, you will see the twin spires of the old Roman Catholic Cathedral. Nearby is the Guangzhou Binguan (hotel) located next to the Exhibition Building, which used to house the Guangzhou Fair exhibits before new facilities were built opposite the Dong Fang Hotel. Closer in, you will be able to observe the roof of the old Confucian Temple, which became the first Peasant Movement Institute established in China; very close to the minaret is the big bell tower.

The balcony also allows you to observe the buildings in the grounds of the mosque, and there is a good view of the courtyard of the temple and the school, which is used for the education of the Moslem Chinese children.

There is a small tower rising from the balcony; about 30 feet high, it is accessible by an internal spiral staircase and reveals a definite lean. Visitors are sometimes permitted to enter.

The Roman Catholic Cathedral

The twin spires of the cathedral are visible from many vantage points in the city. The best view of it is from the terrace of the Renmin (People's) Mansion. The cathedral, built in Gothic style, was consecrated in 1863; the main structure is 80 feet high, the spires attaining 160 feet. It was closed in 1966 but allowed to reopen in 1979.

Mausoleum of the Seventy-Two Martyrs

The mausoleum is located on Yellow Flower Hill (Huanghuagang) in a park about a mile outside Guangzhou. It commemorates those killed in Sun Yatsen's unsuccessful uprising against the Qing Dynasty in 1911. The monument, a curious mixture of various architectural styles both eastern and western, was built in 1918 from funds subscribed mostly by Overseas Chinese. You will see replicas of the Statue of Liberty, a Versailles pavilion, and an Egyptian obelisk.

Monument to the Guangzhou Uprising

The Monument to the Martyrs of the Guangzhou Uprising, located off Zhongshan Road commemorates the heroism of those revolutionaries slain in the unsuccessful Communist uprising of December 11, 1927. The monument is set in a park possessing artificial lakes, footbridges, and various pavilions. Rowboats may be hired. A special feature is the two slabs inscribed with the calligraphy of Zhou Enlai in memory of the 5,700 who died at the hands of the Guomindang during the fighting.

Yue Xiu Park

Guangzhou's best-known park is Yue Xiu, located a few minutes' walk to the east from the Dong Fang hotel. There is a five-story tower on a hilltop in the park known as the Zhen Hai Hou, or "tower overlooking the sea." The tower dates from the fourteenth century—the Ming Dynasty period—and is the oldest building in Guangzhou; indeed, it is one of the oldest buildings you will see in China. As its name suggests, it was a watchtower guarding the city against invasion. It is now a museum housing porcelain treasures and objets d'art dating from the Han period to the present day.

There is a lake where you may hire rowboats, several Olympic-size swimming pools, steep hills providing the energetic visitor with excellent walks under a prolific growth of trees, a number of lookout points over the city, and at certain times of the year magnificent flower displays.

Some Other Parks

A delightful park is the Liuhua Gongyuan (Park of the Stream of Flowers) which is on the westerly side of the Dong Fang. It has a number of lakes, pleasant paths along the lakeside, covered walks, and arched stone bridges. There is also a pleasant little restaurant suitable for a quiet lunch (see Liu Hua Restaurant in the "Dining Out" section). The park is a great favorite with joggers.

Another park worth visiting is Dongshan Gongyuan (East Mountain Park), located a fair way from the city center on the western side. As you enter, you are confronted with rows of palm trees, giving the impression of a tropical rather than a temperate garden. There are many lakes in the park, and you may hire canoes to paddle around the shores and under the many humpback bridges. There is also a zigzag bridge passing across one of the smaller lakes and connecting the two shores.

Of particular appeal is the promontory housing the Dong Hu Restaurant. You pass through an elliptical moongate set in a white wall capped by orange glazed tiles. The restaurant is to your left, but continue straight ahead to the small pavilion. It is a pleasant place to sit and contemplate. The only sounds you will hear are the cries of children, the squeak of rollicks, and the rattle of wind-blown leaves.

In contrast, *Cultural Park* on Renmin Road is a busy and active center of entertainment for the locals, especially in the evenings. You can watch cultural performances in the outdoor theaters, observe the youth of Guangzhou speeding around the roller-skating rink, take a ride on some fairground-type rotary amusements, peer at the fish in the aquarium, visit one of the seven exhibition halls, or quietly sip *cha* in one of the teahouses. It is an interesting place to watch the people in a setting where they tend to be off guard.

Perhaps the most pleasant garden in the city is the Guangzhou *Orchid Garden,* especially for those who want to get away from it all. Only a few minutes' walk from the Dong Fang Hotel and located off a small lane opposite the entrance to Yue Xiu Park, it is a peaceful haven despite its proximity to the noisy traffic of Liberation Road. The thick stands of bamboo, the groves of rare trees, and the lush tropical foliage filter out the hum of traffic, leaving you free to wander in quiet solitude or to sit peacefully on the veranda of the teahouse feeding the golden carp. There is a gazebo at the far end of the garden overlooking a lilychoked pond. Look carefully at the opposite shore and you will see hidden in the foliage a small stone pagoda.

Old Guangdong University

The university site now houses the Lu Xun Museum and the Guangdong Provincial Museum. It is located north of Wen Ming Lu Street not far from the Provincial Revolutionary Museum.

The original university was established in 1924 by Dr. Sun Yat-sen, and in 1926 the name was changed to the Zhong Shan University in his honor. Lu Xun, one of China's foremost revolutionary writers, became head of the Literary Department of the University in 1927 and worked and lived in the Bell Tower Building, which is now a museum devoted to his works. Many meetings of the Guangzhou branch of the Chinese Communist Party were held in the Bell Tower Building during the revolutionary period. The museum was established in 1958.

Zhong Shan University (Old Lingnam University)

This university is one of the oldest and largest in Guangzhou. Visitors to the Canton Fair will usually have an opportunity to go there when the regular soccer matches take place on Sundays at the University's outdoor stadium. The University provides a range of courses, the best known of which are in liberal arts, natural science, and medicine.

Guangzhou Zoo

Guangzhou Zoo is worth a visit; it is probably the best one in China and boasts such animals as the panda and the golden monkey. The zoo is open from 7:30 A.M. to 5:30 P.M. There is also an establishment selling food, so that you can spend the whole day watching the animals if you wish.

Observatory

Guangzhou has a fine observatory, and it is sometimes possible to visit it, particularly if you are in a delegation with a special interest in astronomy or other scientific subjects. Ask your CITS guide.

EXCURSIONS FROM GUANGZHOU

If you have traveled to Guangzhou by train, you cannot have failed to notice the scenery of Guangdong Province. It is one of the most beautiful provinces in China, and you should try to make time available for an excursion to some of the areas located in the countryside.

One favorite is White Cloud Mountain, or Bai Yun Shan, about nine miles northeast of the city. The best way to get there is by taxi, and you need only an hour or two at the most for this excursion. The peak is just over 1,400 feet high and commands a fine view over the town and the Pearl River Delta. The mountain was once a religious center, and many magnificent temples were established on its slopes. These have long since been abandoned or destroyed, but the temple sites have been used for the construction of buildings which serve mainly as health resorts.

If you wish to travel a little further afield, you will appreciate a journey to Conghua, about two hours by car from the city. It is located on the west bank of the Liuxi River at the foot of the pretty Qingyun Mountains; it is a verdant area with luxuriant stands of bamboo. You can take many pleasant walks along the river and in the woods, and when the water level is high enough you can even swim off the river bank. Most people visit there to rest awhile and to enjoy the hot spring a few miles to the north. The guest house at the hot springs has spacious rooms with huge step-down bathtubs, and provides enormous towels to wrap yourself in after you have taken a mineral bath.

An excursion popular with visitors is the trip to *Fo Shan,* some ten miles southwest of Guangzhou. It was once a well-known religious center and is called Buddha Hill after the statue standing on a small hill in the town. The pottery of Fo Shan was known over a thousand years ago. The sites of several kilns dating from the Song Dynasty have been excavated.

Fo Shan was once a more important town than Guangzhou and is reputed to have had a population of about one million. It is still an important industrial town, although the population is now only a third of what it was centuries ago. The main industrial activity is still the manufacture of pottery, and visitors are usually given the opportunity to inspect the Shi Wan pottery factory. There is also an interesting museum which was once a Taoist temple (Zumiao).

Another place worth a visit is the *Seven Star Crags* near Zhaoqing, located about 60 miles southwest of Guangzhou—but the drive takes about three hours one way. You will pass through some fine scenery on the way and be rewarded on arrival with magnificent mountain views. The landscape resembles a miniature Guilin, and photographers delight in the mist-shrouded mountains and rivers. Dinghu a few miles downstream is particularly pretty.

PRACTICAL INFORMATION FOR GUANGZHOU

FACTS AND FIGURES. At 23° 07′N 113° 15′E, Guangzhou is at approximately the same latitude as Havana, Cuba.

It is 1,150 miles south of Beijing by air; 3 hours' direct flight; 1,440 miles south of Beijing by rail, 34–35 hours' train journey; 965 miles southwest of Shanghai by air, 2 hours' direct flight; 1,135 miles southwest of Shanghai by rail, 35 hours' train journey.

Guangzhou is 50 feet above sea level.

Weather patterns are indicated in the table below:

	Jan.	April	July	Oct.
Av. daily maximum temperature (°F)	65	77	91	85
Av. daily minimum temperature (°F)	49	65	77	67
Av. number of days with rainfall	7	15	16	6
Av. monthly rainfall (inches)	0.9	6.8	8.1	3.4

WHEN TO GO. Guangzhou is in a subtropical weather belt. In summer it is hot and humid and the rainfall heavy, with numerous thunderstorms. No pronounced winter season exists; although occasional days can be very cold, generally winter is mild and pleasant. In spring the weather starts to get warmer and the humidity higher; the rainy season begins in April and continues through September, about 80 percent of the yearly average of 64 inches falling in these six months. Autumn is a delightful season with warm days, low humidity, and infrequent rainfall.

The province is frequently affected by typhoons in August and September. Northerly breezes prevail October through February; southerly winds are more evident in the other months.

The most pleasant time to visit Guangzhou is October through March.

WHAT TO WEAR. Light and informal clothing is suitable in Guangzhou. Men do not need a jacket or tie; women are most comfortable in cotton dresses or lightweight slacks. In the winter months the temperature may drop suddenly, and it is useful to have a sweater handy.

In the rainy season (April-May) an umbrella is essential, but, if you have failed to bring one, you can purchase another very cheaply at the hotel shop or in the department store.

Generally speaking, ladies' clothing should not be too revealing.

HOW TO GET THERE. If you are traveling to China to attend the Guangzhou Fair, you would normally enter China through Hong Kong. However, if you are planning your own itinerary, there are a number of alternatives, depending on your international route and ultimate destination. For example, you may want to make Guangzhou (Canton) the last stop on your tour. If so, you can fly directly to Beijing or Shanghai, then proceed south. You can also fly directly to Beijing from Europe or even take the train from Moscow to Beijing. If you are coming from Australia or southeast Asia, convenient stopover points are Hong Kong, Manila, or Bangkok.

GETTING TO AND FROM TRANSPORT TERMINALS. Guangzhou air terminal is about 15 minutes' drive from the city. As there is no bus service, you must take a taxi. Normally though, you will be in the hands of your guide, who will arrange transport and include the fare in the overall cost of visiting Guangzhou.

Guangzhou railway station is close to the city center and only a few minutes' taxi ride from most hotels. Again, there is no regular bus service except the shuttle bus service for guests at White Swan hotel.

Visitors attending the Guangzhou Fair who arrive by rail will normally be transported by bus to their hotels rather than by taxi, since the number of arrivals is too great for the taxi service to handle. The bus service to hotels operates only during the Fair.

HOW TO GET AROUND. By Taxi: Taxis are normally available outside your hotel. The fare charged depends not only on distance covered plus waiting time, but also on the type of taxi, e.g., 4-passenger or 5-passenger vehicle. The dispatcher at most hotels will speak English and will send the taxi to the destination you require. However, some hotels do not have a dispatcher, in which case taxis must be arranged for at the reception desk.

Always carry small notes and change; your driver will often not be able to change large notes. If you forget, you will be delayed while your driver tries to get change from a nearby shop or pedestrian. You may ask the driver for a receipt if you wish; they do not usually provide the "bus-ticket" receipts so common in Beijing.

Of course, you should *never* offer a tip.

Public Transport: Guangzhou also has an efficient system of public buses and trolley buses. They look a bit dilapidated, they are crowded, and their wooden seats are not exactly inviting, but they do (sometimes) get you where you want to go. An English-language map of bus routes is available at your hotel. This form of transport is recommended for adventurous people who are not in a hurry and who can overcome the language barrier.

On Foot: Taking a stroll in Guangzhou is a good way to get a feel of the Chinese way of life in a big city. If you have a sense of adventure, wander where you like, at any hour; you will be perfectly safe. The large avenues are lined with banyan trees, the smaller streets flanked by cool arcades where shops spill their wares out onto the footpath. The streets are crowded, so don't try to hurry. There are myriads of small lanes to explore where you will find small factories turning out their merchandise side by side with herbal tea shops and covered markets bulging with grains, spices, and vegetables.

Take a stroll along the river's edge in the center of the city, along what used to be called "the Bund," and watch the great variety of river craft go by.

If you wish to walk in well-established areas, try the parks and gardens or the zoo.

A really unusual stroll for the early riser is in the meat and vegetable market, where you will find a vast array of produce and a fascinating display of fresh vegetables, meat, poultry, seafood, spices, to name just a few items. The market opens around 4 A.M. but is still bustling at 5 A.M.

  RADIO AND TELEVISION. For those visitors who speak Cantonese, the People's Broadcasting Station in Guangzhou broadcasts on 1060 kilocycles Mondays through Sundays from 5 A.M. to midnight.

Programs in the national language are broadcast on another unit of the Guangzhou People's Broadcasting Station.

If you have brought your radio you will be able to pick up AM and FM broadcasts beamed from Hong Kong, as well as overseas services of the "Voice of America" and the BBC.

Guangzhou has a television station, and if you wish to watch Chinese programs ask your hotel service desk and they will make the necessary arrangements. Video replays of Hong Kong television programs, in English and Cantonese, are also shown at some hotels.

HEALTH. There are no real health problems associated with a visit to Guangzhou. Sometimes the change in diet may bring minor stomach upsets, but these can be controlled readily by the usual remedies.

If you do fall ill and require medical attention, your hotel will assist you to the *First People's Hospital of Guangzhou,* telephone 8642, or the *First Hospital of Guangzhou Medical College* (Foreigners' Outpatient Clinic), telephone 70371.

WHAT TO SEE. The major event of the year is the *Guangzhou Fair,* held every year between 15 April-15 May and 15 October-15 November. A walk through the display areas of the Fair is a good way to gain an appreciation of the variety and quality of the products from China's agriculture and industry. There are also many working models of China's commune systems and oil-producing installations. There are also many films depicting China's agriculture and industry.

Sha Mian has a great appeal to the visitor. It is an island made from a sandbank situated near the Renmin Bridge and was established from 1861 as a foreign enclave, mainly British and French. Today the buildings remain, though in shabby condition, but it is pleasant to stroll down the wide boulevards and tree-shaded walks. The White Swan Hotel is located there.

There are a number of museums in Guangzhou, the most interesting of which is the *Guangzhou Museum* located in the Watchtower overlooking the sea on top of the hill in Yue Xiu Park. The museum houses a fine collection of porcelain treasures dating from the Han period to the present day.

The Peasant Movement Institute is considered to be the Chinese Communist Party's first ideological training school. Mao Zedong and Zhou Enlai both worked here. The Institute, housed in a fine Ming Confucian temple, was converted into dormitories, dining halls, and libraries; these were used by the peasants who were training at the Institute and later sent out into the countryside to spread Communist ideology.

The *Lu Xun Museum* is devoted to the life and works of China's revered socialist writer. There is a particularly interesting series of photographs on display.

Alongside is the *Guangdong Provincial Museum,* featuring a small but interesting display of art treasures that have been excavated in the province.

The only pagoda in the center of the city is the *Decorated Pagoda,* located inside the grounds of the *Temple of the Six Banyan Trees.* The best view of the pagoda is obtained from the minaret of the *Huaisheng Mosque* about half a mile away. The minaret stands in the grounds housing what is said to be the oldest mosque in China, although the existing buildings are modern and of little architectural interest. However, the minaret does offer perhaps the most interesting bird's-eye view of the city because it is central to most of the major sites.

You may attend religious services at the *Roman Catholic Cathedral,* located near the Renmin Hotel.

The *Sun Yatsen Monument* is a fine-looking, elegant building with a blue glazed tile roof. It was built in 1925 after the Chinese revolutionary's death. There is a statue of him in the garden. The building now houses a theater which can seat more than 5,000 people. Another monument, dedicated to those members of the Canton Commune who were killed by the Guomindang in 1927, is the *Mausoleum of the Martyrs of Guangzhou Uprising.* It is a vast tumulus surrounded by a marble wall and containing the remains of the victims.

Above all, Guangzhou is a city of parks and gardens, and you will see there some of the finest in all China. It is pleasant around the artificial lakes and amidst the flower gardens of such well-known parks as *Yue Xiu,* the *Liu Hua,* and the *Dong Shan Park.* Perhaps the most delightful of all is the *Orchid Garden,* which is one of the most tranquil havens you could hope to find in the middle of any city in the world.

The *Cultural Park* is an interesting place to visit, for here you will see the Chinese enjoying themselves in a carnival-ground atmosphere. In particular it is pleasant to watch the Cantonese boys and girls roller skating. In the evenings there are outdoor theaters providing entertainment with the performance of songs, dances, and revolutionary opera.

Other interesting places to visit are the *Old Guangdong University,* the *Sun Yatsen University* located across the river from the city, and the *Observatory.*

The best panorama of the whole city is provided from the lookout point of *Bai Yun Mountain,* about thirty minutes' taxi ride away from the center of Guangzhou.

 MUSEUMS. The *Guangzhou Museum* is located in a five-story pavilion on a hilltop in Yue Xue Park known as the Zhen Hai Lou, or "Tower Overlooking the Sea."

The tower dates from the fourteenth century, Ming Dynasty period and is the oldest building in Guangzhou. It was rebuilt as a lookout post in 1686. It is a rectangular building with a roof separating each story and an exterior painted dark red. The upper roof line has been beautifully restored and there are fine examples of roof figurines on the eaves. On the upper floor there is a balcony overlooking the city. You also look down onto a stadium which has been cut out of the hillside and is reminiscent of a Roman amphitheater. The balcony is a pleasant place to rest and take tea.

In the first section of the museum there are maps and models of Guangzhou, prehistoric tools, fine Han Dynasty tomb figurines excavated near Guangzhou, bronze bells, lacquer ware, bronzes, textile fragments, particularly silk, coins, wooden tomb figures, an iron sword, iron spades, and sets of weights.

From the Sui and Tang periods there are further fine examples of tomb figurines, some of western merchants; "tribute" of silver ingot; gold and silver coins from Persia; pottery found in Guangzhou; a model of the Guang Xiao Temple (it is said that the town of Guangzhou did not exist when this temple was founded in the fourth century).

From the Song and Yuan periods there are an example of Su Dong Po's calligraphy from the Temple of Six Banyan Trees; rubbings from a tablet indicating that a merchant from the South Seas had given money for a Taoist Temple to be restored; good examples of pottery; engraved bricks; a compass; a model of the Temple of the Six Banyan Trees Pagoda.

The museum is closed on Mondays.

Guandong Provincial Museum is housed in a building next to the Lu Xun Museum and located in the old Guangdong University, north of Wen Ming Lu Street. It is open from 8 A.M.–noon and 2–8 P.M.

Outside the entrance is a large iron cannon used during the Opium Wars and alongside it a huge lump of iron used to cast cannons in Foshan. The cannon dates from 1843.

Inside the museum, the first items on display are old fossils and bones that have been unearthed around Guangzhou and in the province. There are also exhibits of weapons, spearheads, and agricultural implements, and some rare pottery fragments.

There is a fine collection of bronzes from the Western Zhou period; a particularly fine example of a *huang* with an animal-head spout and the lid and handle in animal shape; a bell from the Spring and Autumn period; a set of bells used as a musical instrument. From the Warring States period: swords, axeheads, and spearheads. From the Han: an iron sword, Foshan clay miniatures of peasants in the fields, ceramic models of miniature houses with people inside, a ceramic model boat with sailors on board, a set of ceramic musicians, and a fine collection of glazed pottery. From the Southern Han: glazed pottery and some interesting examples with crackled glaze finish. From the Tang: two large urns; from the Yuan: a bronze block used for printing money.

From the Ming: coins embedded in coral and found in the South China Sea; blue and white porcelain, particularly bowls and cups; celadon dishes; jade carvings; stone chops; and cotton fabrics and skirts.

From the Qing: blue and white porcelain urns; tricolor pots; very fine examples of terracotta figurines along with proportionately sized stove, beds, desk, chair, gong, sedar chair, and umbrella.

Lu Xun Museum is located at the Old Guangdong University site where Lu Xun once taught. The exhibits are housed in a building which is immediately before the drive leading from the entrance gates. The museum is open from 8 A.M.–12 noon and 2–8 P.M.

The museum features many excellent photographs of China's revered revolutionary writer and of the towns in which he lived. He was born in Shao Xing (home of China's famous red wine) in Zhejiang Province, and in 1891 went to Nanjing to receive his early education. In 1902, when he was 21 years old, he went to Japan to study for a short period, but most of the time between 1919–1926 was spent in Beijing and Amoy. He went to Guangzhou in 1927 to become head of the Literary Department and lived in the Bell Tower building, now the museum devoted to his life and works. There are some fine photographs depicting the turbulent political situation in the province in 1927. There are also many exhibits associated with Lu Xun's stay in Shanghai and his activities there between 1927 and 1936, the year of his death.

 SHOPPING. Visitors attending the Guangzhou autumn and spring Fairs should make full use of the retail shops in the fairgrounds: there are stores selling down products, silks, textiles, embroidery, fur coats, leather jackets, fur products; there is also a general retail store selling items such as wine, teas, and confectionery. There is a bookstore stocking a wide range of scrolls, art books, paper cutouts, and general literature. Another store sells parkas, ski wear, duvet comforters, and sleeping bags.

Visitors to Guangzhou who are traveling outside the Fair period will probably first choose to visit the *Friendship Store* set aside for foreign visitors. It is located in the four-story building to the left of the Bai Yun Hotel. There you may purchase a wide range of goods; foodstuffs, wines, teas, candy, dried fruits, knitted goods, silks, cottons, brocades, handkerchiefs, scarves, umbrellas. You can also buy suitcases and other luggage items at the store—a useful thing to keep in mind, since you are liable to purchase many items during your travels in China and will probably need additional tote bags. Also on display are shirts, blouses, pajamas, and toys.

You may purchase scrolls, lacquer ware, cloisonné ware, pottery, and porcelain, and you will find a fine range of jewelry. These items are most suitable as gifts; they vary from inexpensive to high-priced, but their main convenience stems from their lightness in weight and small size, always an important consideration for the traveler. One section of the store sells a range of imported cosmetics, wines, spirits, cigarettes, and groceries. There is even a supermarket which stocks imported coffee, powdered milk, insecticides, sanitary napkins, shampoos, deodorants, and many other foreign-brand products. Prices are high.

You may also wish to visit the *People's Department Store,* or *Nan Fang Da Sha,* where you will find hats, shoes, clothing, textiles, sporting goods, bicycles, spare parts, radios, TV sets, towels and linen, to name just a few items. It is well worth going into this store and browsing around, particularly to watch the Chinese shopping. As a visitor you may purchase any of the items on display in the shop, even cotton goods (which are rationed throughout China) without handing over the ration coupons. There is an excellent and inexpensive optical service: imported frames are available at low prices but prescribed lenses take about a week. A branch of the Friendship Store is also located within the People's Department Store.

LOCAL PRODUCTS. Should you wish to browse in the small shops specializing in locally made products, you could well commence by taking a taxi to the intersection of Beijing Road and Zhong Shan Road. In the streets forming this intersection you will find stores selling everything from safety pins to color television sets. In this busy thoroughfare there are shops selling herbs, pharmaceuticals, rattan ware, basket ware, stone chops, stationery, birth control pills (no prescription needed), books, wall posters, second-hand clothes, household items, brooms, ropes, paints, brushes. The streets are bustling and noisy; there is a great deal of traffic and incessant honking of horns. The crowd spills out on to the roadway, since there is rarely enough room on the footpaths to make one's way.

 ANTIQUES. If you are shopping for antiques, you should visit the *Guangzhou Antique Shop* located at 146 Wende Road (telephone 31 241 or 34 229). Here you will find a good range of antiques and reproductions, but the strong emphasis is on pottery and porcelain ware. There is a limited range of scrolls; also old and new jade, rather unusual natural stone chops, and Qing reproductions of ancient bronze ware.

For serious collectors the *Antique Warehouse* in Hongshu Road is definitely worth a visit. This is a dusty, attic-like shop, and you will have to poke around and climb ladders, so wear your oldest clothing. If you envisage purchasing antiques for export totaling more than, say, $2,000, you may request the management of the Antique Warehouse to take you to the *Guangzhou Antique Export Company,* also in Hongshu Road. Payment at this shop is by letter of credit, not cash. This means that the goods cannot be taken with you but must be consigned for export.

If you are spending quite a few days in Guangzhou and have some time to spare, you may like to visit a busy and interesting shopping area not far from the center of the city; it is in *Xiu Li Er Road.* Fairgoers often make use of the services of two tailor shops located there; their work is good and inexpensive. One is the *Guangzhou Tailor Shop* and the other the *Nan Fang Tailor Shop.* You will need to be staying in Guangzhou for at least 5–10 days to make use of their services. The Guangzhou shop does the usual range of tailoring, while the Nan Fang does shirts and blouses only. It is customary to bring an item that the shop can copy; they do not usually measure clients, and when they do the results are often disappointing.

There are many interesting shops in the area selling pottery, herbs, medicines, meat, and flowers.

Documentation: Every antique sold should have a red seal affixed. You should insure that your purchase is recorded on your currency declaration form or you will not be able to take the antique out of China.

USEFUL ADDRESSES AND TELEPHONE NUMBERS

International calls:	
operator,	08.
information,	30000.
Calls within China:	
long distance operator,	03.
long distance:	
information,	06.
Guangzhou: directory assistance	04.
Telephone call charges,	33440.
China International Travel Service (CITS),	33454, 61451.
China Travel Service (CTS),	32247, 31862.
Public Security Bureau (Foreigners' Section),	31060.

Air Services

CAAC (General Administration of Civil Aviation China), Liuhua Square (opposite Railway Station): International Passenger Service, tel. 34079, 33684. Domestic Passenger Service, tel. 31271. Cargo Service, tel. 33590. Information, tel. 31034.

Banks

Bank of China: Guangzhou Branch, 137 Chang Ti. Cable: Chungkuo Guangzhou. Telex: 44074 BKCA CN, 44075 BKCA CN. Tel. 20543.

Bookstores

Foreign Language Bookstore, Beijing Road. Tel. 32734.
Xinhua Bookstore, 276, 280, and 296 Beijing Road. Tel. 30873.

Canton Fair

Foreign Trade Center, Renmin Bei Rd. Tel. 30849.
Executive Office, Haizhu Square. Tel. 23800. Cable: CECFA or 0700 Guangzhou.

Cinemas

Guangzhou, 65 Yanjiang Yi Road. Tel. 88205.
Xinhua, 76 Zhongshen Road V. Tel. 32292.
New Star (Xinxing), Zhongshan Road V. Tel. 32366.
Dongshan, Zhongshan Road II. Tel. 77539.
Golden Voice, Xiuli Road I. Tel. 25936.
Honan, Hungteh Road. Tel. 50420.
Yunghung, Beijing Road. Tel. 32630.
Xihao, 24 Xihao Ermalu. Tel. 85557.
Xinwen, 186 Beijing Road. Tel. 30721.

Department Stores and Shops

Friendship Store, Yanjiang Road I. Tel. 22018.
Jiang Nan Native Produce Store, 399 Zhongshan Road IV. Tel. 31207.
Nan Fang Department Store, 49 Yanjiang Road I. Tel. 86022
Guangzhou Antique Shop, 146 Wendebei Road. Tel. 31241, 34229.
Guangzhou Antique Warehouse, 575 Hongshu Bei Road. Tel. 87600.

Hospitals

The First People's Municipal Hospital, Ren Min Road (North): Emergency ward, tel. 86421.
The Second People's Municipal Hospital, 63 Xinfeng Road: Emergency ward, tel. 86711.
The Chinese Medicine Hospital, 16 Zhuji Road. Tel. 86111.
The Hospital attached to *Guangzhou Municipal Medical College,* 151 Yanjiang Road. Tel. 20518.

Hotels

Dong Fang, Ren Min Road (North). Tel. 69900.
Bai Yun, Huan Shi Road (East). Tel. 67700.
Hua Chiao, 2 Qiaoguang Rd. Tel. 61112.
Guangzhou, Haizhu Square. Tel. 61556.
Guangquan (Hot Springs) Villa, San Yuan Li. Tel. 61334.
Liu Hua, Ren Min Road (North). Tel. 68800.
Ren Min, 207 Changti Road. Tel. 61445.
Sheng Li, Sha Mien 54. Tel. 61223.

Parks

Guangzhou Cultural Park, Xiti Ermalu. Tel. 87232.
Guangzhou Zoo, Xianlie Road. Opening Hours: 7.30 A.M.–5.30 P.M. (Ticket counter closes at 4.30 P.M.). Tel. 75574.
Li Wan Park, Xiangyang Road. Tel. 87880.
Liu Hua Park, Xicun Highway. Tel. 35238.
People's Park, Zhongshan Road V. Tel. 34843.
Dongshan Lake Park, Dashatou. Tel. 75672.
Yue Xiu Park, Jiefang Road. Tel. 30876.

Photo Studios

Kun Lun Photo Shop, Ren Min Road (South). Tel. 25636.
Yang Fang Photo Shop, Zhongshan Road V. Tel. 31206.

Post and Telecommunications

Guangzhou Cable Bureau, Zhongshan Road III. Tel. 71617.
Guangzhou Cable Bureau Changti: 30416. Long Distance Calls, tel. Ex.03. Information, tel. Ex.04. Service, tel. Ex.05.
Guangzhou Post Office, Yanjiang Road I. Tel. 86615.
Guangzhou Telecommunications Bureau, Liu Hua Square. Tel. 77623, 75190.

Rail Services

Guangzhou Railway Station, Liuhua Square, Ren Min Road (North). Tel. 33333.

Restaurants

Banxi, 151 Xiangyang Yi Road. Tel. 88706, 85655, 87031, 87255, 86505, 88105.
Beijing, 10 Xihao Ermalu. Tel. 87694, 85690, 87158.
Beixiu, 899 Jiefang Road. Tel. 35941, 32281.
Beiyuan, 318 Dengfeng Bei Road. Tel. 30087, 32471, 33365.
Caigenxiang, 167 Zhongshan Liu Road. Tel. 86835.
Datong, 63 Yanjiang Yi Road. Tel. 85933, 88697, 86396, 87345.
Dongjiang, 337 Zhongshan Si Road. Tel. 35343, 35568.
Dongshan, Yimalu Dongshan Guigang. Tel. 78553, 76108.
Dongfang Hotel, Xicun Highway. Tel. 69900.
Guangzhou, 2 Wenchang Nan Road. Tel. 87136, 87840.
Huabei, 247 Zhongshan Wu Road. Tel. 33837, 34417.
Jingji, 8 Shamian Er Street. Tel. 88784, 85790.
Nanyuan, 120 Qianjin. Tel. 51576, 50532.
Shahe, 79 Xianlie Dong Road Shahe. Tel. 75449, 75639.
Snake, 41 Jianglan Road. Tel. 21811, 22517, 23424.
Taiping, 344–346 Beijing Road. Tel. 35529, 31147.
Taotaoju, 228 Xiuli Yi Road. Tel. 87306, 85769.
Wild Game, 249 Beijing Road. Tel. 30997, 30337.
Yuyuan, 90 Liwan Road. Tel. 86838, 88552.

Theaters

Friendship (Youyi), People's Road North. Tel. 33402.
Red Flag (Hongqi), 250 Zhongshan Road IV. Tel. 34073.
Nanfang, 88 Jiaoyu Nan Road South. Tel. 30195.
People's (Ren Min), 292 Damalu, Changti. Tel. 22917.

Theater-Cinemas

Guangming. Nanhua Road Central 116. Tel. 51436.
Yan'an. Yan'an San Road. Tel. 78801.
Xianjin. 441 Xiuli Yi Road. Tel. 85679.

Travel Agents

China International Travel Service 179 Huanshi Road. Tel. 33454.
Ticket Office 61451

Consulates

United States, Dong Fang Hotel, tel. 69900.
Japan, Dong Fang Hotel, tel. 61195.

DONG FANG HOTEL. The Dong Fang is a large, rambling hotel built around a small park with wide well-laid-out gardens and a pond in the inner courtyard. The hotel is centrally located and is only a short walk from the

Guangzhou Railway Station. It is ideal for fairgoers, being on the opposite side of the road to the main entrance of the Fair. Tel. 69900.

Rooms are ¥ 50 per day; suites are available from ¥ 100 and up per day.

The Dong Fang Hotel usually accommodates visitors from English-speaking countries, Western Europe, and South America. There is a sauna, a massage service, and an electronic games room.

There are three main restaurants. The one serving Western food on the ground floor has a decor featuring chandeliers, mirrors, plush carpets, a raised center section surrounded by a fountain, and often entertains guests with live music and entertainment. The main dining room is separated into two areas. The restaurant on the eighth floor serves small portions of average quality Chinese food at standard prices. The restaurant located in the garden area has two sections: one serving Western food, the other Chinese; the standard of both is good. There is an International Club, offering restaurant facilities, a coffee shop, and a disco.

Coffee Shops: Both are located in the new wing: one near the center pond is air conditioned and decorated in modern style; the other, left of the entrance on the ground floor, is austere in decor and features piped music.

Shops: Food shop, 9 A.M.-2 P.M. and 5-8 P.M.; handicrafts shop, 9 A.M.-2 P.M. and 5-8:30 P.M.

Post Office: Weekdays 12 noon-2:30 P.M. and 6-8:30 P.M. (to 10 P.M. during the Fair) and on Sundays 6-8:30 P.M. only (to 10 P.M. during the Fair).

Cables: Weekdays 12 noon-2:30 P.M. and 6 P.M. to midnight. Sundays 6 P.M. -midnight only. (These are Fair hours; in other months, the service times are more restricted.)

Telex: 12 noon-12 midnight (more restricted service outside the Fair periods).

Bank: Weekdays 12 noon-2:30 P.M. and 6-8:30 P.M.; Sundays 6-9 P.M. only.

Beauty shops: 8 A.M.-8 P.M.; men's hairdresser 8 A.M.-8 P.M. There is also a L'Oreal de Paris beauty salon offering a range of services for both men and women.

Billiard room: 9 A.M.-11 P.M. (¥ 3 per hour per table—there are 4 tables). Table tennis room: 9 A.M.-11 P.M.

Consulates: The U.S. Consulate-General (Tel. 69900) and the Japanese Consulate-General (Tel. 61195) are both located in the Dong Fang.

During the Guangzhou Fair (15 April-15 May; 15 October-15 November) other services are available. The Guangzhou Fair Liaison Office No. 1, set up to assist visitors, is open from 8 A.M.-12 noon and 2-6 P.M. (tel. 621), and is usually located on the fourth floor of the old wing. There is also a China Travel Service office, open 8-9 A.M. and 3-7 P.M., located on the 3rd floor of the old wing (room 366; tel. 517).

During the Fair there is a bar/restaurant established on the 11th floor of the new wing, known affectionately to China traders as "Top of the Fang," and open between 8 P.M. and midnight. During the day (2:30-5:30 P.M.) it is a coffee shop, serving coffee, tea, and pastries.

During the Fair only, there is a 24-hour clinic, on the second floor of the old wing, staffed by a doctor and two nurses.

BAI YUN HOTEL. (tel. 67700) The Bai Yun (White Cloud) is a new 33-story hotel with 3,250 rooms, all air conditioned, completed in 1977. It is located in the northeast section of the city, and while a little isolated, is quiet and peaceful. There is an inner courtyard just off the entrance lobby which is most attractive, huge natural rocks supporting three large trees have been retained, and a waterfall runs over the rocks into a deep rock pool. Room rates: ¥ 40-120 per day.

A full range of facilities are available at the hotel, and business visitors in particular will find that the range of commercial services are efficiently run. There is a western food restaurant on the ground floor and one serving Chinese food on the first floor. Both restaurants are open during the Guangzhou Fair, but at other times only the first floor restaurant is open, although western food can still be prepared on request.

WHITE SWAN HOTEL. (Tel. 86968; telex 44149 WSH CN; cable 8888). Located on Shamian Island (1 South St.) overlooking the Pearl River, the White Swan Hotel provides five-star international standard accommodations.

Rooms are air conditioned, carpeted, equipped with direct dial telephone service to Hong Kong, refrigerator, color television, and night-table console. The 28-story hotel has four room categories: deluxe double suites, three-room suites, garden rooms, standard rooms.

Hotel facilities include: swimming pool; gym; sauna; beauty parlors; shopping arcade; dancefloor; bars; disco; and 600-seat conference hall. There are two business centers equipped with translators, typists, telex, and cable facilities. The hotel staff is well trained. Dining facilities are extensive, and include three Chinese restaurants, a Western restaurant, a Japanese restaurant, a coffee shop, and a tea house.

The hotel is about a 30 minute drive from the airport and a 15 minute drive from the train station. Guests arriving by train can make use of the reception desk maintained at the station and take advantage of the free shuttle bus provided by the hotel.

Room rates vary according to floor number, view and size—beginning at ¥65 for a double room with island-view on floors 5 to 7, rising to ¥80 for a similar room with river-view on floors 8 to 27. Suites range from ¥120–180 and up.

RENMIN MANSION. This hotel caters for Chinese compatriots from Hong Kong and Macao, overseas Chinese from southeast Asia, and "overflow" guests of American and European origin. The hotel is located at 207 Changti Road (telephone 61 445) and overlooks the Pearl River; for this reason it is usually cooled by a river breeze, a decided advantage in the humid spring and hot summer months. The hotel is divided into two sections, new and old, the new providing better accommodation. The restaurant provides good meals. The hotel also has a hairdresser, retail store, bank, post and telegraph office. Rooms: ¥20–60 per day.

LIU HUA. Located on Renmin Road North (telephone 68 800), this hotel provides accommodation for Chinese compatriots from Hong Kong and Macao, overseas Chinese from southeast Asia, and, on rare occasions, accommodation for Americans and Europeans. The hotel has definite advantages for Fairgoers; it is located on a site adjacent to the fairgrounds and is also conveniently located opposite the Guangzhou Railway Station; on the opposite corner is the main office of the post and telegraph service. The hotel is equipped with a restaurant, hairdresser, retail store, bank, post and telegraph facilities, and bookstore. Rooms: ¥25–75 per day.

GUANOQUAN. This villa is located in Sanyuanli (telephone 61334) and is reserved for distinguished and special Chinese guests from Hong Kong and Macao. A small hotel, it is luxuriously appointed and particularly well known for its hot spring baths. It has the usual facilities, including a restaurant.

OTHER HOTELS. The following hotels are used to accommodate either overseas Chinese from southeast Asian countries or Chinese compatriots from Hong Kong and Macao: *Biejing, Binjiang, Guangdong, Guangzhou, Haizhu, Heping, Hongfeng, Huaqiao, Lanting, Nan Fang, Nanhu, Shamian, Shanzhuang, Shengli, Shimen, Shuangxi, Xihao, Xinhua, Xinshidai, Xinshijie, Xinya, Xuanmen,* and *Yanjiang.*

SPORTS. *Joggers* will find their Chinese counterparts pounding the tracks of Liu Hua and Yue Xiu parks in the early morning. The scenery is tropical, and you will run by the edge of lakes and ponds.

Those visitors wishing to revive memories of an ill-spent youth may retire to the *billiard* parlor of the Dong Fang Hotel, where both billiard and pool tables are to be found and markers are available for solo players.

The Dong Fang also boasts *badminton* courts, set in the hotel inner garden, and three *table tennis* tables in a large room adjacent to the barber shop.

DINING OUT. Dining out in Guangzhou is altogether different from dining out in Beijing. For one thing, the style of cooking is different; for another, the setting and decor of some of the restaurants in Guangzhou are magnificent, in contrast to the austerity of Beijing's restaurants.

The description of the dishes is more poetic. How could anyone be more subtle than a chef who describes a dish as "Dragon and Tiger" when he is referring to snake and civet cat? Or "Snake Crossing the Mountain Peaks" for a soup containing meat from the boa constrictor? Or "Fragrant Meat" when referring to dog?

Such dishes are exceptions, not in the mainstream of Cantonese cooking; but the poetry extends to dishes which will find favor with the Western visitor's palate. For example, "A Hundred Flowers Floating on the Lake" is a consommé in which poached quail eggs, decorated to resemble flowers, float on the surface; "Jade Trees" are green vegetables.

Another notable difference is the emphasis given to the appearance of the food. This is nowhere more noticeable than in the presentation of cold hors d'oeuvres, where the foodstuffs will be arranged to form a bird, butterfly, or flower. They will be distributed to provide not only an appropriate color but the right textural appearance as well. Stand up and take a good look at this when it is served. You will often feel it is too attractive to break up for serving.

Keep your eyes open when the other dishes are served. You will often notice the decorative touch that has been deftly applied; a fine example is the filigree carving on the top of the melon used as the bowl in presenting the famous winter melon soup. There is a host of other examples.

The Cantonese restaurants have been divided into various categories to help you make a choice. Recommended banquet menus are also provided for your guidance. You will note that we used the words "Canton" and "Cantonese" in this section. These have been adopted because they have become internationally accepted in relation to Chinese cuisine. And the word "Canton," despite its association in the Chinese mind with foreign exploitation and national humiliation, can be freely used in China, although when speaking of subjects other than cooking it is probably more polite to use the name "Guangzhou." Sometimes a restaurant is listed according to its English equivalent: "Snake Restaurant" is more appropriate for our purposes than "She Can"; so too is "Vegetarian Fragrance" Restaurant rather than "Caigenxiang Sucai." The first section to follow lists a few restaurants that you should perhaps give first preference to if your time is short. Then come lists of the "top ten," specialty restaurants, and so on.

THREE BANQUETS IN GUANGZHOU

If your time is short you may not have time to try many of the Cantonese restaurants. Here, then, is a recommendation for a "three-banquet" stay in the city. Gourmets should remember that a banquet can be prepared for lunch as well as for dinner. The restaurants have been chosen on the basis of their preparing the best food available in Guangzhou in magnificent surroundings. They are: Nan Yuan (South Garden Restaurant), 151 Xiang Yang Rd. 1, Tel. 50532, 50542; Ban Xi, Tel. 85655; Bei Yuan (North Garden Restaurant), 318 Dengfeng Beilu, Tel. 32471.

It would be hard to find three better Cantonese restaurants anywhere in the world.

For advice on recommended banquet menus you should consult the section devoted to this subject. You should note that one of the best combinations of dishes for a banquet is given for the Guangzhou Restaurant which is not listed above (its setting is not as good as the others) but is listed in the "five banquets" list which follows.

FIVE BANQUETS IN GUANGZHOU

If you have sufficient time for five banquets, you should also consider: Guangzhou Restaurant, 2 Wenchang Lukou, Tel. 87136, 87840, 23493, and Datong (Great Harmony Restaurant), 63 Yanjiang Rd., Tel. 88697, 86983, 20318.

The banquet menu selected for the Guangzhou is one of the finest you will ever experience. The Datong is an excellent restaurant affording a view on one side of the terrace of the city and on the other of the Pearl River and its busy boat traffic.

THE TOP TEN RESTAURANTS OF GUANGZHOU

Address	Restaurant	Telephone
Ban Xi	Small Brook (literally "Half	85655
151 Xiang Yang Rd. I	Stream") Restaurant	88706
		87031
Bei Yuan	North Garden Restaurant	32471
318 Dengfeng Beilu		33365
Datong	City of Datong Restaurant	85365
63 Yanjiang Rd.		85396
		85505
		85933
Dongfang	Easterly Restaurant	69900
Dong Fang Hotel		
Renmin Rd. North		
Dongjiang	East River Restaurant	35568
337 Zhongshan Si Lu		35343
Dongshan	East Mountain Restaurant	70556
Dongshan Gueigang		76108

Guangzhou	Guangzhou Restaurant	87136
2 Wenchang Lukou		87840
Nan Yuan	South Garden Restaurant	50532
120 Quianjin Lu		50542
Shahe	River Sands Restaurant	75639
79 Xianlie Dong Rd., Shahe		70956
		78850, Ext. 214
Yu Yuan	Happy Garden Restaurant	88552
90 Liwan Nanlu		88369
		86838

er hu
(2-String Fiddle)

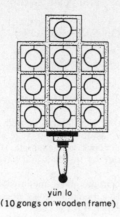

yün lo
(10 gongs on wooden frame)

NAN YUAN

南园酒家

前进路120号

电话：50532,

50542

South Garden Restaurant

Qianjin Lu, 120

Telephone 50532

50542

The South Garden restaurant is a good fifteen minutes' taxi ride from the Dong Fang Hotel but well worth the effort. You arrive to find a glade hidden behind a white wall topped with green glazed tiles. Inside is one of the most beautifully landscaped greeneries you will ever see: bamboo groves, camphor trees, flowering vines, and colorful orchids set amid ponds and running brooks. There are small dining pavilions with finely worked colored glass windows, deep blues and whites predominating. The setting is perfect for serving the exquisite food prepared by the chefs of this restaurant.

The menu below would be suitable for 8 guests and would cost about ¥45 per person, not including drinks.

多色冷拼盘	Hors d'Oeuvres Platter
玉液鱼蓉羹	Jade Sauce on Fish Soufflé Soup
北京片皮鸭	Peking Duck
双色酝鸡夹	Two Style Chicken Platter

松子鲜鲈鱼	Steamed Pomfret (Fish) with Pine Nuts
金风明虾卷	Golden Prawn Rolls
广州炒饭	Fried Rice Guangzhou Style
两甜点心	Two Types of Pastry

A specialty is the Assorted Cold Platter served to commence the meal. A variety of meats, poultry, seafoods, and vegetables are put together to represent a butterfly or peacock, for example. The dish is typical of the Cantonese approach to cooking: food should have visual appeal as well as satisfying the taste buds.

A specialty not included in the above menu is Mao-tai Chicken; this dish, as the name suggests, has a pungent flavor derived from the famous and potent Chinese liquor in which it is cooked.

BEI YUAN

北园酒家	North Garden Restaurant
登峰北路318号	Dengfeng Beilu, 318
电话：32471	Telephone 32471, 33365

The North Garden restaurant is set in an old teahouse enclosing a series of ornamental pools connected by paths and framed by stands of tropical plants and fine gardens.

The menu presented below is suitable for four persons and costs about ¥40 per person, not including drinks.

鸡丝鱼翅	Chicken Shreds with Sharksfin Soup
花雕肥鸡	Shao Xing Chicken
油泡虾球	Sauteed Prawn Balls
脯鱼鲜蘑	Sliced Fish Filet with Straw Mushrooms
炸蟹钳	Crab Balls
菜远鱼球	Fish Filet in Wrapped Ham with Vegetables
咸点心：两种	Dim Sum, two kinds: Shrimp Toast, Baby Spring Rolls

甜点心：两种   Dim Sum, two kinds: Pastries for Dessert

干烧伊面   Soft Noodles

A specialty of the restaurant is the famous Sharksfin Soup with Shredded Chicken. Sharksfin is a delicacy in China, and in this dish it is combined with shredded chicken to form a subtly flavored broth. Usually a small bowl of pink-colored vinegar is placed alongside your plate; you should add a little to your sharksfin to bring out the subtlety of the flavors.

Another specialty, Shao Xing Chicken, is cooked whole in the Hua Diao brand of Shao Xing red wine. It is served sliced, and possesses a special fragrance and subtle sweetness.

Another excellent dish is Chopped Crab Balls. The crabmeat is finely chopped and compressed, then deep-fried. It is served with the small piece of claw protruding.

BAN XI 泮溪
(Small Brook [literally "Half Stream"] Restaurant)

荔湾东路   151 Xiang Yang Rd. I

电话： 85655   Telephone 85655, 88706, 87031

From the outside, this fine restaurant resembles a vast private residence. Inside, the dining rooms are situated in rambling teahouses spread around a small lake. One section of the restaurant is even located on a floating houseboat. You should take the opportunity of strolling around this land-scaped garden restaurant, following the zigzag paths up and down, over bridges, across ornamental lakes, alongside bamboo groves, and through stands of tropical foliage. The center piece is a three-story teahouse with upswept eaves, traditional Chinese roof, and decorated window glass in deep blues and white.

Although the restaurant caters for a vast number of guests, the atmosphere is dominated by the beauty of the surroundings. However, as you would expect from one of Canton's finest restaurants, the dishes prepared and served there match the images that greet the visitor. Nor is the comfort of guests forgotten: there is a section which has been modernized and includes air-conditioning, a facility visitors appreciate in the hotter, more humid months. But since this section was more recently built you will be sacrificing old-world charm for modern comfort.

The menu presented below would be suitable for 10–12 guests and costs about ¥50 per person, not including drinks.

象生大拼盘   Assorted Cold Hors d'Oeuvres Platter

蚧肉烩瑶蛀   Dried Scallop and Crab Soup

脆皮炸子鸡   Crispy Skin Chicken

香美带皮虾   Sweet Soy Prawns (with Shells)

碧绿生鱼球	Fish Filet with Green Vegetables
五彩大鸭丝	Breast of Duck with Spring Onions and Silver Sprouts
鲜笋炒鸽片	Sauteed Pigeon Slices and Bamboo Shoots
锅炒鹌鹑蛋	Quail Eggs on a Bed of Green Vegetables
炒饭	Fried Rice
咸点： 五彩玉绣球 蜂巢王芋角 珍粉千层酥 玉液锅贴包	Dim Sum, four kinds: Shrimp Balls, Stuffed Meat Pastry Shells, Baby Spring Rolls, Small Dumplings.
甜点： 可可核仁战 莲蓉麻堆仔	Dessert, two kinds: Red Date Cakes, Sesame Balls
水果： 鲜木瓜和天津梨	Fruits: Fresh Papaya and Tientsin Pears

The first dish, the Hors d'Oeuvres Platter, is worth standing to look at. It is always beautifully decorated in the form of a bird, butterfly, or a similar object.

The Scallop and Crab Soup is prepared with shredded dry scallops, a Chinese delicacy, and shredded crabmeat in a chicken stock, cooked with herbs and mixed with eggwhite.

Another specialty is Quail Eggs on a Bed of Green Vegetables. Quail eggs are a Cantonese specialty. They are served hard-boiled after having been cooked with shrimp roe. The sauce is also derived from shrimp roe. The color, smooth texture, and taste of the quail eggs contrast with the flavor of young green vegetables.

GUANGZHOU

广州酒家	City of Guangzhou Restaurant
文昌路2号	Wenchang Lukou, 2
电话： 87136	Telephone 87136
87840	87840

This restaurant is located in the Shui Li Er Road area, described in the Guangzhou "Shopping" section, in a rambling old teahouse with many staircases and terraces. Foreign visitors dine upstairs, where there is a maze of landings with individual dining salons located on the various terraces. It is a noisy, animated place with the central courtyard overlooked by verandas on each floor. When you look down from your own veranda you will see room after room of diners and hear the chatter, laughter, and clink of plates rising from the floors below.

The banquet menu presented below has some of the finest dishes you are likely to encounter in China. It is suitable for about 10–12 persons and costs about ¥50 per guest, not including drinks.

八宝冬瓜汤	Eight Treasures in Winter Melon Soup
广州文昌鸡	Wenchang Chicken Guangzhou Style
双拼片皮鹅	Roast Sliced Goose
百花煎酿鸭掌	Webbed Feet of Duck Stuffed with Shrimp
清蒸边鱼	Steamed Fish with Scallion and Black Beans
岭南烧乳鸽	Lingnan Braised Quail
香葱炒蚧	Sautéed Crab with Scallion
烧鸡腿拼田鸡腿	Braised Meats of Chicken and Frogs' Legs
油泡鲜虾仁	Sautéed Shrimp
广州炒饭	Fried Rice Guangzhou Style
干烧伊面	Soft Noodles
甜点两式	Desserts: Two Pastries with Water Chestnut Cream

The opening dish is a Cantonese specialty. Eight Treasures in Winter Melon Soup is served in a hollowed-out melon. The top of the melon is carved in a filigree effect, and the translucent melon meat contrasts with the dark green of the skin, giving the effect of a magnificent jade carving. The first course is the soup itself with the eight delicacies, which include game, chicken, ham, mushrooms. For the second course the flesh of the melon is scooped away.

Braised Meats of Chicken and Frogs' Legs are served off the bone, cut into very thin slices, and presented in layers on a bed of jade-green vegetables. A fine sauce is poured over the meat to create a subtle difference in flavor.

In Webbed Feet of Duck Stuffed with Shrimp, chopped shrimp is placed on cooked skin from the feet of the duck and molded to resemble a flower.

When this attractive and tasty dish is served it resembles a platter of small flowers.

Roast Sliced Goose is a famous Cantonese specialty. It is moist, succulent, and not oily; the skin is crisp, and the overall flavor is sweet. This is goose at its best.

A specialty of the restaurant which is not included in the above menu is an hors d'oeuvre consisting of a large dish of Whole-Boiled Shrimp cooked with the shells on and eaten with various sauce dips. This is a seasonal dish and when available is in great demand.

DONGFANG

东方宾馆   Easterly Hotel Restaurant

人民北路   Renmin Beilu

电话 69900   Telephone 69900

The private dining rooms are located on the eighth floor of the Dong Fang hotel and are next to the large restaurant used during the Fair by guests in transit and foreigners temporarily resident in China. All banquets held in the private dining rooms must be ordered 12–24 hours in advance.

The menu presented below costs about ¥35 per person, not including drinks, and would be suitable for 10 guests.

现拼彩盘   Assorted Cold Hors d'Oeuvres Platter

片大红乳猪   Roast Suckling Pig

炒桂花鱼翅   Sharksfin with Eggs

炸竹笋脆虾   Prawns with Bamboo Shoots

鲜蘑扒鹌蛋   Straw Mushrooms Sautéed with Squab Eggs

湖上漂海棠   Floating Flower Soup

东江盐烤鸡   Salt-Baked Chicken

杏仁甜奶露   Almond Cream

锅贴饺子   Jiao Zi (stuffed dumplings)

干烧伊面   Soft Dry Noodles

Roast Suckling Pig is a specialty of this restaurant. The whole pig is cooked on a spit and the skin glazed with honey, plum, and soy. Then the skin is separated from the fatty layer beneath, cut into small squares, and put back in place on the carcass. The pig is then served whole on a platter. The skin is eaten by dipping each square into plum sauce and then wrapping it with some scallion in a crepe-like pastry. When the skin has been eaten, the remainder of the pig is removed to be cut up, then returned as a separate dish.

Sharksfin with Eggs, or "Cassia Flower with Eggs," as it is known in Chinese, is another specialty. Sharksfin is usually served in a soup, but is prepared here with eggs. The dish is both delicious and visually appealing: the meat is translucent in contrast to the eggs, which are fluffy yellow.

Salt-baked Chicken is a well-known Cantonese dish. It is wrapped in clay and baked in salt. The dish is served with the skin and meat cut into slices. The name stems from the old days when beggars, who had no pots, cooked chicken in the earth.

Floating Flower soup is a consommé in which poached quail eggs, decorated to resemble flowers, float on the surface. This is another example of a dish which is both a visual delight and a fine gastronomic experience.

DATONG

大同酒家   Great Harmony Restaurant

沿江路63号   63 Yanjiang Road

电话: Telephone 85365, 85396, 85505, 85933

The Datong Restaurant is located on the top floor of the building on the Bund (now known as Yan Jiang Road). On entering the building you will be taken to the restaurant in an elevator, and on the top floor you will walk down an aisle past the "masses" section of the restaurant, then down a flight of stairs to an open terrace. There you will find dining rooms for foreign visitors.

There is a fine view of the Pearl River from the terrace and you will see the busy river traffic. In the evening you will feel a cool and refreshing breeze from the river, a welcome relief from the heat and humidity present at certain times of the year.

There are also a fountain and fish pond with a small stone bridge crossing to one of the dining rooms. Altogether it is a pleasant, elegant, small restaurant with exceptionally good food.

The menu below is suitable for 8-10 guests and costs about ¥45 per person, not including drinks.

鲜虾冬瓜粒   Winter Melon Soup

开屏孔雀鸡   Peacock Chicken

油泡生虾仁   Sautéed Shrimp

鲜菇乳鸽片	Sliced Squab with Mushrooms
学九王三丝	Sautéed Spring Onion with Chicken and Ham Shreds
松子炸鱼	Whole Fried Fish in Plum Sauce and Pine Nuts
翠竹生虾扇	Green Vegetables with Shrimp
炸蛋菀柱	Fried Quail Eggs with Diced Pork
饺子	Jiao Zi (stuffed dumplings)
咸点三式： 　虾馅饺子 　肉馅饺子 　小春卷 （宴会开始时吃）	Dim Sum, three kinds of salty ones: Shrimp Dumplings, Minced Pork Dumplings, Tiny Spring Rolls (all served at the beginning of the banquet)
甜点三式： 　宴会结束时吃	Three kinds of sweet pastries served at the end of the banquet

Cantonese cooking is renowned for its *Dim Sum,* which literally means "touch the heart." These are bite-sized morsels of exquisitely prepared dumplings and are a favorite in teahouses in China.

In the menu above the dim sum is listed last. However, the salty ones are usually served at the beginning of the meal and the sweet ones at the end after the *jiao zi,* a meat-filled dumpling.

A specialty of this restaurant is Peacock Chicken. The braised chicken is cut up and presented in the form of a peacock with its fan opened. It is served with vegetables and ham.

Another specialty is Straw Mushrooms on Crab, which is not included in the above menu. The restaurant picks the plumpest, juiciest mushrooms, sautés them with spices, and serves them on a snow-white bed of shredded crabmeat with a cream sauce. It is a delicious and almost sensual dish; regrettably, it is seasonal.

YU YUAN

愉园饭店	Happy Garden Restaurant
荔湾南路90号	Liwan Nanlu, 90
电话：88552	Telephone 88552, 88369, 86838

The Yu Yuan is located in a fairly new building: there is an attractive modern entrance opening into a center courtyard which features a rock garden and fish pond surrounded by tropical foliage. Foreign visitors dine in the upstairs dining rooms which are fairly noisy but have a festive atmosphere about them.

The menu presented below costs about ¥50 per person, not including drinks, and would be suitable for 10–12 guests.

八宝冬瓜汤	Eight Treasures in Winter Melon Soup
北京烧烤鸭	Peking Roast Duck
金华碧绿鸡	Ham and Chicken Meat on Green Vegetables
鲜笋鱼肉球	Fish Balls with Bamboo Shoots
银针乳鸽丝	Squab Slices with Silver Bean Spouts
鲜虾扒草蘑	Straw Mushrooms with Shrimp
香麻百花糕	Fragrant Sesame Flower Cakes
京北酥鱼肉	Northern Pepper Fish Filet
炒饭	Fried Rice
面条	Noodles
鹌蛋奶露	Egg Custard Cream with Quail Eggs
四式美点	Four Kinds of Pastries

A specialty on the above menu is Squab Slices with Silver Bean Sprouts. The squab meat is cooked off the bone, sauteed, and served on a bed of bean sprouts which have had the pointed head and tail portion clipped off so that the remaining slender portion resembles a "silver needle." The meat is tender and the flavor subtle. There is an excellent contrast in the softness of the meat and the crispness of the bean sprouts.

Peking Roast Duck is not a specialty of Canton, but for those visitors who are going to this city only and will not have the opportunity to travel north, this restaurant presents a good opportunity to taste the famous dish. The chef will personally bring it to the table to show the guests. Then he will carve the crisp skin from the meat, cutting it into small squares. You may then take a few pieces of skin with your chopsticks and dip them into the rich brown sauce provided, add some chopped scallion, and wrap the garnished skin in thin crepes or pancakes. The stuffed pancake is usually eaten with the fingers. After the skin has been eaten, the carcass containing the meat of the duck is taken away and carved up by the chef, then served for eating either in the small pancakes or without embellishment.

At this restaurant the Winter Melon is often not carved for presentation unless you make a specific request.

DONGJIANG

东江饭店	East River Restaurant
中山四路337号	337 Zhongshan Si Lu
电话：	Telephone 35568, 35343

Located in the center of Guangzhou, this restaurant serves excellent food in simple surroundings. Foreign visitors eat upstairs in the first floor dining room where most tables are separated from each other by screens. There are only a few tables located in private dining cubicles.

The menu presented below is suitable for 6 guests and costs ¥40 per person, not including drinks.

雪耳川虾丸海棠蛋	Snow Mushrooms with Quail Egg Soup
盐烤鸡	Salt-Baked Chicken (house specialty)
烧酰明虾拼乳鸽	Stuffed Giant Prawns and Roast Squab
碧绿鸡丝扒鲜菇	Chicken Shreds with Mushrooms on Bed of Green Vegetables
韭王生鱼球	Fish Filet with Spring Onions
豉椒炒肉蟹	Crab with Black Bean Sauce
东江炒面	Dongjiang Fried Noodles
新疆哈蜜瓜	Sinjiang Honey Melons

Braised Duck stuffed with eight delicacies and glutinous rice is the other specialty, although it has not been included in the menu. It is a richly flavored and succulent dish. Guangzhou is more famous for its goose dishes, and the duck dish at this restaurant is a rather unusual exception.

Other delightful dishes in the menu are Stuffed Giant Prawns Served with Roast Squab and Crab Pieces in Black Bean Sauce (in season), both these dishes may be eaten with the fingers.

DONGSHAN

东山饭店	East Mountain Restaurant
东山龟岗	Dongshan Gueigang
电话： 70556	Telephone 70556, 76108

The restaurant is located about fifteen to twenty minutes' ride by taxi from the center of the city. The area you pass through on your way is rarely seen by foreign visitors and presents one of the most picturesque night scenes you will come across in Guangzhou.

On arrival you will see two large trees outside the restaurant in a street that is cobblestoned and dimly lit; it is faintly reminiscent of the old sections of Paris. You walk up stone steps to the entrance and will be ushered to the second floor where there are dining rooms for foreign visitors.

The menu presented below would be suitable for 4 guests and would cost ¥35 per person, not including drinks.

七彩冷拼盘	Assorted Cold Platter
雪耳炖鹌鹑	Baby Quail and Snow Mushroom Soup
煎酙大明虾	Giant Prawn with Soy and Ginger Sauce
红烧海狗鱼	Seal Stewed with Mushroom
烧松子鱼	Whole Fried Squirrel Fish
鸡丝烩伊面	Soft Noodles with Chicken Shreds
咸点心： 荸荠肉丸	Dim Sum: Shrimp-filled Puff Pastry, Water Chestnut Meat Balls
甜点二式	Dim Sum: Two Kinds of Sweet Pastry

A feature of the Assorted Cold Platter is the magnificent visual arrangement of the food. The meats, poultry, and vegetables are laid out to represent, for example, a bird or butterfly. The foodstuffs are also placed on the plate to convey a realistic texture to the animal or flower represented.

The Whole-Fried Squirrel Fish is unusual in the way it is served. It is prepared for deep frying by cutting the surface of the skin to form a diamond pattern. During the cooking process the surface forms small cubes which separate from each other. The texture is firm but the juices are retained inside the cubes. It is a most unusual way to prepare fish, and you are recommended to try this dish.

The Seal Stewed with Mushrooms may present difficulties for Western visitors, but if you are seeking something unusual, leave it on the menu. The taste is somewhat similar to chicken but with a slightly firmer texture.

SHA HE

沙河饭店	River Sands Restaurant
沙河大街	79 Xianlie Dong Rd., Shahe
电话：	Telephone 75639, 70956

This restaurant is located in an old building without distinctive features, except for the many flights of steep stairs you will have to climb. Consequently, only the strong-limbed should make the effort. The dining rooms for foreign visitors are located around the small terrace, where you may sit at a ceramic table and take tea before eating. The rooms themselves are not particularly attractive but are quiet.

The name of the restaurant is derived from *ho fan,* the Cantonese name for flat rice noodles. These are the specialty of the restaurant and are served at the end of the banquet. There are four or five different types served with different toppings. You will never taste noodles anywhere in the world quite like these; they are reputedly made using only water from the springs of nearby White Cloud Mountain. Many believe this restaurant has brought the art of preparing noodles to a peak of perfection. Certainly, many Cantonese Chinese who live outside of China make a pilgrimage to this restaurant when they return to their homeland just to taste the magnificent noodles. No better recommendation can be made.

The normal range of Cantonese dishes, prepared to an excellent standard, is available at this restaurant as a forerunner to the noodles course.

The tea prepared here is reputed to be brewed also in White Cloud Mountain spring water.

"HIDE-AWAY" RESTAURANTS

Sometimes you wish to escape from your group and be alone for a while. Here are five restaurants where you can "hide-away."

The first, **Northern Beauty,** is a delightful little spot a few minutes' walk from the Dong Fang Hotel. But don't imagine you can "escape" by going to this restaurant during the Canton Fair—better try one of the other four.

The **Economy** is a pleasant little place and convenient if you wish to dine there after exploring Sha Mien Island.

At the **Taiping** you get loads of food, and at the **Liu Hua** the chefs specialize in fish and seafood. The **Dong Ho** is better known for its setting than for the food.

NORTHERN BEAUTY

北秀   Northern Beauty Restaurant
                              (or Bei Xiu)

解放路   Liberation Road, 899

电话：30941   Telephone 30941, 35941, 32280

The restaurant is very close to the Dong Fang Hotel (about 3 minutes' walk) and is therefore popular with Fair-goers. If you are going to the restaurant from the hotel, turn right on leaving the exit gate and walk to the main road (Liberation Road) about 150 yards away. Follow the road to the right for about 200 yards; you will recognize the restaurant by the large number of bicycles parked nearby, hence the name "The Bicycle Restaurant" given it by the China traders.

Go up the stairs to the top landing on your left. You may eat either in the large dining room or on the terrace. The terrace is particularly attractive, though noisy, during the warmer weather; in the evening colored lights in the surrounding trees are turned on, and the effect may provide you with a fleeting memory of a small Mediterranean restaurant. Across the road there is an open-air cinema and you can glance across and catch glimpses of the Chinese movie being shown. The interior salon is furnished with dark wooden chairs and tables, and the atmosphere is cool and somber; there are large overhead fans to keep the air circulating.

Presented below is a luncheon menu for two which costs about ¥15 per person, not including drinks.

百花香酥鸭	Fried Duck Stuffed with Minced Shrimps
炒油菜	Sautéed Green Vegetable
清蒸鲈鱼	Steamed Perch with Scallion, Leek and Black Bean

The restaurant is well known for its Sunday brunch, which features an excellent variety of dishes at a most reasonable price. The brunch menu presented below is suitable for a minimum of 4 persons and costs about ¥18, not including drinks. You must place your order the night before; this can be done through your hotel lobby desk.

鲜虾云吞	**Shrimp Wonton**
莲煎软饼	Fried Soft Lotus Cake
香脆马蹄糕	Fragrant Crisp Waterchestnut Cake
雀巢鹌鹑蛋	Quail Eggs in a Nest
鸡粒稻儿饼	Chopped Chicken Biscuit
脆皮鲜虾煎饼	Crispy Shrimp Pancakes
鲜虾梅花饺	Shrimp *jiao zi*
伊面	Soft Noodles (optional)

LIU HUA

流花饭店	Liu Hua Restaurant
流花公园	Liu Hua Park (Renmin Rd., N.)

Telephone 68800

The Liu Hua Restaurant is located in the park of the same name situated on the western side of the Dong Fang Hotel. If you enter the park by the corner entrance opposite the Dong Fang, take the path that runs to the left along the edge of the lake; turn right following the shoreline and you will come to a gateway. Go through the gateway and along the path to the two-story building ahead, and go to the top story of the building where foreign guests eat.

The dining room is noisy, but you will have a pleasant view through the full-length window of the tropical foliage that grows in abundance around the restaurant.

It specializes in fish, mostly freshwater types, and seafoods, especially prawns, squid, and shrimp. Pork and beef dishes are also available.

Try the *Wanyu,* which is a fresh-water fish caught in the nearby lake; it is a specialty of the house. The Fish Balls with Sesame Seeds are also excellent.

ECONOMY RESTAURANT
(JINGJI)

经济餐馆   Economy Restaurant

沙面   8 Er Ma Rd., Shamian

电话： 88784   Telephone 88784, 87790

This tiny restaurant is situated on Sha Mian Island, which used to be the foreigners' enclave from the 1860's onwards. The restaurant is a pleasant place to visit for lunch or dinner after you have spent a few hours exploring the island.

Whether on foot or in a taxi, you will cross the small bridge at the eastern end of the island. Then continue straight ahead for about three or four hundred yards until you come across a cross street called Sixth Street; turn right into this street, and about 20 yards down on the right-hand side you will see the restaurant entrance. There is a large camphor tree just outside.

The section for foreigners is upstairs in two small rooms, each accommodating two tables and overlooking a small courtyard with a tree growing in the center. You might easily imagine that you are in New Orleans.

The luncheon menu presented below is suitable for two people and costs about ¥22 per person, not including drinks.

椒子牛肉   Sliced Beef with Green Chili Pepper

香煎明虾录   Sautéed Prawns (with Shells)

烤禾花鹊   Rice Birds Stuffed with Liver Sausage

清蒸鲈鱼   Steamed Perch with Pork and Mushroom Shreds

水果   Fresh Fruits

A specialty of the restaurant is Rice Birds Stuffed with Liver Sausage, a dish that is seasonal. These tiny birds are caught in the rice fields in nets during the autumn. After preparation they are cooked whole and sometimes stuffed with a type of liver sausage, as in the dish on the menu above, and are eaten whole, the bones being softened during the cooking process.

They are a delicacy in South China and represent for most foreign visitors a new gastronomic experience. If in doubt, try a small plateful for your first order.

TAIPING 太平

北京北路344号   344 Beijing Beilu

电话: 35529   Telephone 35529, 31147

The Taiping is situated in one of the busiest sections of the city and was once a restaurant in the Lam Brothers chain, which operated in Guangzhou, Hong Kong, and Macau prior to World War II.

Foreign visitors eat on the third floor, and there are numerous steep flights of stairs to climb before reaching the upper landing. There you will be shown into a large dining hall which has two large tables, each suitable for about ten guests, and six small tables seating 4–6 people. The dining hall is not subdivided into smaller banquet rooms. The tables at the rear are pleasantly situated near the windows and are cooler; you look out over miniature trees which decorate the window sills and down onto the tops of tall trees growing in the nearby park.

The restaurant is suitable for banquets and also for couples who may wish to dine alone, although it certainly lacks privacy. The menu presented below is suitable as a lunch for two and would cost about ¥20 per person, not including drinks. There is also a Western menu.

菜青炒鸡球	Sautéed Chicken with Green Vegetables
脆皮火鹅	Crispy Skin Roast Goose
茄汁鱼块	Fried Fish Filet with Plum Sauce

We have listed below some of the best dishes from the restaurant menu suitable for a banquet. You should make a selection from the major dishes according to the number of guests, and have the restaurant recommend the supplementary courses.

姜汁焖鲤鱼	Carp Baked with Ginger and Scallion
蚝油焖鸡	Whole Chicken Baked in Oyster Sauce
炸脆皮鸡	Crispy Skin Chicken
金华玉树鸡	Chicken Slices in Aspic and Ham on Bed of Green Vegetables
四色扒鸭	Braised Garnished Duck
拆焗鸳鸯鸭	Boned Duck Stuffed with Minced Shrimp

果汁煎鹅脯   Sliced Goose in Plum Sauce

清蒸鲈鱼   Steamed Perch in Ginger and Scallion

姜葱炒蟹   Braised Crab in Ginger and Onion

蟹钳竹笙   Crab Balls with Bamboo Shoots

油泡虾球   Sautéed Prawns

百花酎北菇   Mushrooms Stuffed with Shrimps

韭黄虾丸   Shrimp Balls with Spring Onions

DONG HE RESTAURANT

东河饭店   East River Restaurant

东山公园   Dong Shan Park

This is a lunchtime restaurant (closes at 2 P.M.) located in Dong Shan He Park (East Mountain River Park) in a modern building on the edge of the lake. You enter the grounds of the restaurant through an elliptical moongate set in a white wall. Inside there is a large ornamental pool let into the floor and a tall stand of bamboo growing up through the cutaway ceiling. The restaurant opens onto a patio where there are gardens and shade trees, and from the patio there are steps leading to the edge of the lake.

While the setting is both modern and pleasant, you can expect to find chrome chairs with vinyl covers and see a plastic tablecloth laid out before you, a disappointing contrast with the natural beauty outside.

The food is basic and rather similar to that served in one of the "masses" restaurants. There is no menu so you must be guided by the waiter. Some English is spoken.

SPECIALTY RESTAURANTS

SNAKE RESTAURANT (SHE CAN)   蛇餐馆

江南路 41 号   41 Jianglanlu

电话：   Telephone 81811, 83424, 82517

Strictly for the adventurous and those with an iron stomach. The Cantonese love snake dishes and are just about the only people in China who eat such food.

When you arrive at the restaurant you will be confronted at the entrance by a shop window filled with writhing snakes. There are hundreds of them, including the deadly cobra. As you stand watching this bed of coiled venom, the snakes will ignore you, but tap on the window and they will flick their tongues at you. It is not the most inviting welcome you will receive at a Chinese restaurant, but it's probably the most unusual one.

As you walk up a few flights of stairs to the foreign visitors' section, you will note that the restaurant is packed with diners eating the various snake specialties.

When you are seated at your table, and before you begin your meal, you should, if your taste is so inclined, order snake bile. These cost ¥25 for three from ordinary snakes—more from rare snakes. You can also ask to see the bile sac removed from a snake while you sit at your table, an operation you will not see in many other places in the world. One of the snake men from the restaurant will arrive with a basket of snakes and squat down beside you. He will take a snake from the basket, place one foot gently on its head and the other gently on its tail, and feel along about one-third of the length of the snake from the tail end until he finds the bile sac under the skin. You may, if you wish, also try to locate it by running your thumb along the snake's cold, clammy underside.

Once the bile sac is located, the snake man slices into the skin, using a thin blade, and with a quick movement of the fingers squeezes the bile sac from the body and severs it. He then places the bile sac on a small saucer and returns the snake, seemingly undisturbed by this 30-second operation, to the snake basket, selecting another one for the next bile sac extraction.

The snake man repeats this operation as often as necessary to remove a sufficient number of bile sacs for the attendant guests. The bile is squeezed from the sac and is served mixed with Maotai in a small glass. The beverage has the reputation, probably unfounded, of being good for the heart and also for virility.

You may also ask to see the snake you are about to consume skinned before your eyes. This operation is not for the faint-hearted, but it has the advantage of being over in about 20 seconds. As far as can be determined there is no advantage for the snake.

The snake man takes the snake destined for your table from the basket, puts its head gently under his foot, and, holding the snake up by the tail, runs a thin blade the full length of its body. He severs the head and pulls the skin from the snake's body, leaving a writhing, headless and skinless carcass. It is not the most pleasant way to begin a meal, and you will probably have visions of the operation while you are eating. Of course, you may prefer to dispense with the whole performance and concentrate on the delicacies on the menu.

The menu below is suitable for 8–10 people and costs about ¥40 per person, not including drinks. If you indulge yourself by drinking snake bile, the cost will increase according to the number of bile sacs purchased and the rarity of the snake from which they came.

三蛇鸡肉汤   Chicken Soup with Three Kinds of Snake

蛇肉丸   Snake Meat Balls

著名脆皮鸡   Crispy Skin Chicken

过山峰炖清汤   Clear Broth of Big Mountain Snake (Boa Constrictor)

菠罗梅酥鸭	Duck Breast in Plum Sauce and Pineapple
软炸大虾	Deep Fried Prawns with Flavored Salt
香菇鸭掌	Straw Mushrooms with Duck Pieces
蚝油花雀	Stuffed Rice Birds in Oyster Sauce
广州炒饭	Cantonese Fried Rice
水果	Fresh Fruit

A specialty of the restaurant is Chicken Soup with Three Kinds of Snake. This is a tasty broth with the meat of three deadly snakes mixed with chicken meat and flavored with spices. Obviously, the venom is removed from the snake prior to cooking; otherwise there would be few people remaining who could testify to the existence of the restaurant. It is traditional when serving this dish to garnish each individual bowl with petals from the chrysanthemum flower.

Another specialty is Clear Broth of Big Mountain Snake, which is made from the meat of one or more of the large snakes, particularly the boa constrictor, that live in the south of China. This is a delicately flavored broth and slightly sweet.

A specialty of the restaurant not on the above menu is Dragon and Tiger Stew. The real name of this dish is the "Struggle of the Dragon and the Tiger," referring to a well-known Chinese myth concerning these two animals. The "dragon" is in fact snake and the "tiger" is civet cat, prepared together in a thick soup which is almost like a stew. It is a famous dish in Canton.

VEGETARIAN FRAGRANCE RESTAURANT

中山六路167号	167 Zhongshan Liu Lu
电话: 86836	Telephone 86836, 86835

Vegetarians on a tour of Guangzhou will be delighted to find this fine restaurant where, of course, there are no meat dishes. The dining rooms for foreign visitors are upstairs. On entering you will notice that the walls are paneled in bamboo, the tables and chairs are made of bamboo, and your dining room is separated by a bamboo wall in which there are fan-shaped windows.

The banquet menu presented below makes an interesting change. Although the dishes are all made of vegetables, they are prepared in such a way that you will be certain you are eating succulent meats or seafoods. It would be suitable for 4 persons and could cost ¥35 per person, not including drinks.

清汤雪耳	Snow Mushroom Consommé
晁湖上素	Vegetables from Chaohu Lake

玉宇葵花	"Sunflower of the Universe"
菜元扒鲜菇	Vegetable Balls
葵花扣豆腐	"Beancurd Covered by Sunflowers"
六宝大拼盘	Dish of Six Treasures
凤凰鲜奶露	"Phoenix Milk Cream"
炒饭	Fried Rice
美点二式	Desserts

The Snow Mushroom Consommé is a soup made from the woodear, a flower-like fungus which is translucent and almost silver. It is a rare delicacy, and in the consommé has an exquisite flavor.

Another specialty, the Dish of Six Treasures, is usually served at the beginning of the meal, and features vegetables which are cooked and prepared to provide the appearance, texture, and taste of various meats such as duck, chicken, sausage, and meat balls.

WILD FRAGRANCE (GAME) RESTAURANT (YE WEI XIANG)

北京路	249 Beijing Lu
电话：30337,	Telephone 30337
30997	30997

This restaurant, located in an old building in Beijing Road, is crowded and noisy. Foreign visitors eat in the upper floor section, again under crowded conditions; but if you like game and exotic seafood such as turtle, this is the place for you.

The menu presented below costs about ¥35 per person, not including drinks, and would be suitable for 8–10 guests.

鸡丝烩鱼肚	Shredded Chicken with Fish Maw
碧绿花子鸡	Chicken with Green Vegetables
雪花野鸭片	Sliced Wild Duck
鸡油武昌鱼	Whole Wuchang Fish
翡翠生鱼球	Fish Balls in Jade Vegetables

香肠肚花鹊	Sausage Stuffed with Meat of the Lark
瓦罐香狗肉	Fragrant Dogmeat Stew
锦绣鹧鸪丝	Sautéed Quail Slices
云腿丝拌片	Yunnan Ham Slices
咖啡鲜奶露	Coffee Cream Soup

One specialty of this restaurant is Fish Balls in Jade Vegetables. The meat from the fish is chopped up with water chestnut and other delicacies. The dish when served resembles a platter of small round flowers, the bed of green vegetables representing the leaves.

The dish for the adventurous is Fragrant Dogmeat Stew, which is cooked in an unglazed earthenware pot with soy sauce, ginger, wine, and various spices. The dish tastes very much like stewed beef but is more fragrant. The color of the meat is brownish-red through absorption of the wine and soy. Traditionally chefs may prepare this dish only from young black dogs.

Although not listed on the menu above, another specialty of this restaurant is Civet Cat.

**yue qin
(Moon Guitar)**

SHANGHAI

Notorious Past, Stable Present

Shanghai's history and way of life are dominated by the river—not the nearby Yangzi, as many visitors suppose, but the Huangpu or Yellow River (not the same as the giant Yellow River in northern China), a wide stretch of brown water bearing a variety of craft ranging from ocean-going vessels to single-oared sampans. Shanghai, which means "up from the sea," overlooks a bend in this river where there are sailing craft and power vessels navigating the difficult waters side by side. Even the city's local name stems from a river: it is known to the Chinese as "Hu," from the word *hudu,* a name given in an old legend to the lower reaches of the narrower Suzhou River which also runs through the city and empties into the Huangpu.

Shanghai is one of the three municipalities, along with Peking and Tianjin, directly under central government control. It harbors China's major port, which extends a total of 35 miles along the bank of the Huangpu. The river waterway is about 200 yards wide and nine yards deep, and is navigable all year round for ocean-going vessels up to 10,000 tons.

Along the river's edge is a boulevard called the Bund—at least, that was its name before 1949—with wide paths and narrow gardens, a cool place during the sweltering heat of summer. Locals go there in the early morning hours to do their *Taijiquan* (exercises), practice their musical instruments, or sing. Make the effort to rise early and join them; and if you have left your violin behind or are not feeling too energetic, simply lean against the river wall and let the sea air envelop you. Close your eyes and listen to the sound of the sirens and horns beating across the water through the early morning mist.

Flanking the Bund are the old European-style buildings that were once the international banks and trading companies. If you look carefully you can still see the old names chipped into the stonework or written in faded paint on the plaster. These buildings now house the Chinese municipal officials, trade negotiators, customs officers, and bankers. In the middle of the Bund stands the Heping (Peace) Hotel, an elegant old building with a pointed bronze-green roof. It was once owned by the well-known Sassoon family of England and called the Cathay Hotel.

Now turn back to the river and take a good look at the river craft. In few places in the world will you see old blunt-nosed steamers side by side with sailing junks tacking against the tide, and ferries with hundreds of passengers jammed between decks passing strings of barges laden with coal. And certainly nowhere else can you see such old vessels still in commission. Some are old museum-pieces with shiny white paintwork while others are rust-buckets ready to slide into the river when the plates finally corrode through. And there are sampans everywhere, whole families manning the single *yuloh* oar when the tide is strong.

From the park you can also see the main shopping street, Nanjing Road, which runs into the Bund quite near the Peace Hotel. Take a stroll there: it is the shopping area which is the most western in style in the whole of China. You will notice there are plenty of shop windows —a feature absent in most of the shopping centers in other Chinese cities—and there is a semblance of window decoration to promote the goods on display. The street is packed with people, and the scene will remind you at once that Shanghai, with its 11 million inhabitants, is the most heavily populated urban area in the world. About six to seven million people live in the city proper in an area as small as 55 square miles.

You will also notice that, while Shanghai is at first sight European in appearance, the foreign architectural influences are mostly restricted to the Bund area. Beyond the façade stretch miles of buildings typical of many Chinese industrial cities: low buildings housing offices, shops, and busy markets. As you proceed further from the center you will come across large industrial areas with factories surrounded by workers' apartment buildings.

Eventually you will come into the area of intensively cultivated agricultural communes supplying fresh vegetables, grains, pork, and other food to the city. The fields are irrigated by canals drawing off water from the network of rivers, creeks, and waterways forming the Yangzi delta. Further to the west are low hills, but you can rarely see them clearly through haze caused by industrial pollution.

The polluted atmosphere of Shanghai is a reminder that the municipality is China's most important industrial base and premier center of trade and industry. Over the years, Chinese planners have developed

Shanghai's light and heavy industry ventures to provide a more balanced local economy, so that the major production sectors are now iron and steel, shipbuilding, chemicals, motor vehicles, heavy machinery, tires, oil refining, petrochemicals, paper, electrical equipment, glassware, and textiles.

Many production centers are located in industrial estates in outlying areas with associated housing developments, shopping centers, hospitals, and schools. One of the most publicized centers is Minxing, about 15 miles south of the city. Another is Pengpu, about three miles north of the Shanghai urban center. The Chinese proudly show visitors these "showcase" centers.

The visitor will soon appreciate that Shanghai, because of its industrial and commercial strength, is probably the most prosperous city in China. You will certainly note that the women are better dressed than elsewhere and are more clothes-conscious, wearing smarter jackets and more colorful floral skirts here than anywhere else in China. Young couples hold hands in daylight, a practice rare in China, and even walk arm in arm along the Bund in the evenings. All this may appear tame to the Western observer, but it is considered quite permissive in most areas of China.

The residents of the city are also well known for their business acumen. China traders will confirm that their dealings in Shanghai are usually handled more efficiently and effectively than in any other city in the PRC, and that the state trading corporation officials there "understand what business is all about." No doubt this native ability has been developed throughout Shanghai's long participation in international trade and commerce.

Shanghai has a rare combination of a violent and colorful past and a stable industrial present. It is the largest metropolis on the Asian mainland and one of the largest in the world. It holds a fascination which stems from its one-time international notoriety and its current place in modern Chinese history as a revolutionary city. When you have been to Shanghai you can boast of having visited the most populous, polluted, and one of the most famous cities in the world.

History

The first recorded evidence of Shanghai is under the Song (A.D. 960–1280), but there is little doubt that a settlement existed well before then. The town was undeveloped under the Yuan (1280–1368), Hangzhou being far more important in that period, and it was not until the seventeenth and eighteenth centuries that trade and commerce began to expand to any large extent. During this period Shanghai became an important cotton-processing center.

During the Opium War, Shanghai fell to the English fleet in 1842 and, following the Treaty of Nanjing, was opened to foreign trade. The English dominated commerce in the region, but American and European traders were also active. All claimed rights to territories where their nationals were subject to the jurisdiction of the Consul and not the Chinese ruler.

Shanghai was threatened by the Taiping armies in 1853 and from insurrection within. Both movements were eventually put down by the combined forces of the Manchu court and the European powers.

By the middle of the second half of the nineteenth century, foreigners dominated Shanghai, controlling banks, customs, trading houses, shipping, and industry. Yet incredible poverty and squalor existed in areas shut away from the magnificent mansions and grounds of the rich. A reaction to this intolerable situation developed among the Chinese working class and intellectuals. In 1921 the Chinese Communist Party was founded in Shanghai, Mao Zedong being one of the founding members. Some years later there were armed uprisings by the working class in coordination with the Guomindang northern expedition. However, the rivalries within the Guomindang broke into the open in Shanghai when Chaing Kaishek put down the Communists and Trade Unionists in a bloody massacre.

Later, during the Sino-Japanese war (1937–1945), Shanghai was occupied by the invaders. After they were expelled, civil war broke out between the Nationalists and the Communists. By 1949 the Communist armies had crossed the Yangzi and the country was in their hands. In Shanghai, as in the rest of the country, the state took control. Private property and businesses were nationalized and the remains of the previous order swept away. Very few foreigners stayed behind to witness the changes. An industrialization campaign was undertaken and heavy industry developed—shipbuilding, iron and steel, heavy machinery. At the same time, light industry was stimulated, particularly the production of pharmaceuticals, electrical equipment, machine tools, chemicals, and tires.

Shanghai's port facilities were developed. About half of all Chinese exports now pass through the port. With this development has come a growth in Shanghai's commercial sector, so that it is now the most important trading and commercial center in China.

EXPLORING SHANGHAI

The facade of inner Shanghai has changed little since the Communists began to govern the country in 1949. The same buildings are there; but their use is different. The banks flanking the Bund now house Chinese officials, part of the old British Consulate is the Seamen's Club and Friendship Store, the racetrack has become a park, the golf course a zoo, and the palatial villas of the rich have been transformed into "children's palaces," schools, playgrounds, nurseries, and hospitals. The once notorious "Blood Alley" is now a quiet shopping street.

The Bund

Your first wish will no doubt be to take a stroll along the Bund (Zhongshan Road) and through the small parks along the river's edge. Here you will see citizens of Shanghai at rest, exercising, reading or practicing musical instruments.

You may wish to put your elbows on the sea wall and watch the bustle of the river traffic, one of the most interesting river scenes you will see anywhere in the world: a blending of power and sail on a highly congested waterway. You will be fascinated by the navigating maneuvers of diverse craft.

On the other hand, you may wish to lean your back against the sea wall and study the buildings opposite. Probably the first building you will notice is the Peace Hotel with its pointed green tower. Once the most palatial hotel in the East, as its former name, Cathay Hotel, suggests, it is almost a museum piece of the dignified but old-fashioned architecture that can now be found only in cities like Vienna, Paris, and some of the East European capitals.

Next to it, to your right, is the Bank of China, almost exactly the same height but without the tower. The four other buildings about half the height of the Bank and also to your right were formerly old banks and trading companies; they now house the Chinese state trading corporations which are solely responsible for the import and export of goods and commodities to and from all foreign countries.

About one-third of a mile to the left stands the Customs Building, with a tower more than 100 feet high housing an enormous clock that chimes each quarter of an hour to the refrain of "East Is Red." Next to it stands a lower but wider building with a small dome on top; this is the Shanghai Municipal Committee Headquarters, which houses the cadres responsible for administrating the municipality and which was "under siege" during the Cultural Revolution.

Nanjing Road

While the Bund is Shanghai's most interesting street, Nanjing Road is its busiest. Here you will find the city's shopping area extending for some miles, a multitude of shops on each side of the tree-lined boulevard, separated here and there by restaurants, cinemas, and theaters.

Nanjing Road also leads to Renmin (the People's) Park and Square, which was formerly the Shanghai Race Course. The park is well kept, has a vast expanse of lawn, and possesses a great many trees to protect you from the summer heat. To the west of the park is the Shanghai Municipal Library, built in the 1850's.

You will notice that the main streets running north and south, like the Bund, are named after the provinces of China, while those running east and west, like Nanjing Road, are named after famous Chinese cities.

The Shanghai Industrial Exhibition

The Exhibition, located several blocks further west of the People's Park in Nanjing Road, is housed in a large hall built in the severe architectural style of the Soviet Union. This building, surmounted by a high spire, was formerly known as the Sino-Soviet People's Friendship Building, before the two countries suffered strains in their relationship. A permanent exhibition of Chinese industrial products, mostly made in Shanghai, is held in the building and is of interest to business

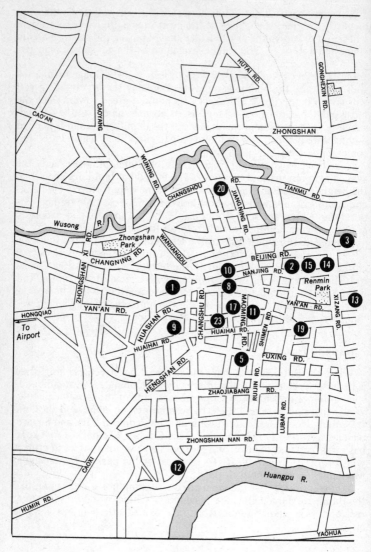

Points of Interest

1) Children's Palace
2) Daguangming Theater
3) First Department Store
4) Former Residence of Lu Xun
5) Former Residence of Dr. Sun Yet-sen
6) Former Temple of Confucius

7) Friendship Store
8) Industrial Exhibition
9) Japanese Consulate-General
10) Jing An Si Temple
11) Jinjiang Hotel
12) Long Hua Pagoda
13) Museum of Art and History
14) Overseas Chinese Hotel

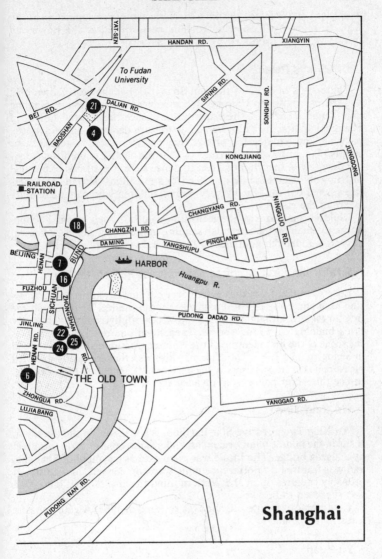

15) International Hotel
16) Peace Hotel
17) Red House Restaurant
18) Shanghai Mansion
19) Site of the First Communist
    Party Meeting
20) Temple of the Jade Buddha
21) Tomb of Lu Xun

22) Temple of the Town Gods
23) United States Consulate General
24) Wu Xing Ting Tea House
25) Yu The Mandarin's Garden

executives and visitors wishing to learn about developments in the
Chinese economy. You will probably be surprised at the range and
quality of goods produced by China's industries.

Children's Palace

There are a number of these in Shanghai, but the best-known one,
and the one shown to visitors, is located near the junction of Nanjing
and Yanan Roads. In these institutions, once the palatial homes of
Shanghai millionaires, children come to learn dancing, singing, music,
painting, and handicrafts, or else they exercise, listen to teachers, or
simply play. From all sides you will hear the chatter of children enjoying themselves, the shuffle of feet in dance steps, the strains of musical
instruments. You may be disturbed by the political slogans and mes-
sages acted out for you by very young children who cannot be fully
aware of the content.

Children may attend these institutes outside their normal school
hours to obtain extracurricular training in music, dance, art, gymnastics, etc., under the guidance of highly trained tutors.

Site of the First Chinese Communist Party Meeting

Located not far from the center of the city, in the old French Concession area and close to the Fuxing Park, the site has become a shrine
in Chinese revolutionary culture. Now beautifully restored, this gray
brick building with four doorways, each with an overhead arch, was
the scene of the first meeting of the Chinese Communist Party founded
in Shanghai on 1 July 1921. You may also visit the beautifully panelled
pleasure boat that was used by the participants, including Mao Zedong,
to flee the secret police who invaded the meeting.

Wu Xing Ting

Wu Xing Ting, or Five-Star Pavilion, is a teahouse in the old town.
It sits in the middle of an ornamental lake and is connected to the street
by a zigzag bridge. The locale was once used as a symbol of Shanghai
and was featured on pottery, ceramic ware, dinner sets, and curios. It
probably conjures up in the Western mind the idea of what old China
was supposed to be like.

The teahouse is quite old and was restored in 1965. A gate opposite
leads to Yu Yuan.

Yu Yuan

You should try to visit Yu Yuan, or "Yu the Mandarin's Garden."
It is characteristic of the architectural style of the Ming and Qing
Dynasties. Its visual beauty captures the essence of landscape art of the
period, creating the impression of maximum space in a small area.

Yu Yuan was built during the years 1559 to 1577 for Pan Yunduan,
a landlord and official of the Ming Dynasty. The garden, reminiscent
of those in Suzhou, features more than 30 halls and pavilions. It is
divided into three parts, each separated by a white brick wall the top

of which forms an undulating gray dragon. Each part of the park, although divided, has a balance and harmony creating a unity of expression.

One of the pavilions, the Hall for Heralding Spring, has a place in revolutionary history. It was the headquarters of the Society of Small Swords that rose against authority in 1853 and eventually fled to Zhejiang (Chekiang) to join the Tai Ping Rebellion. Chen Ah-lin, one of the important leaders of the Society, used the pavilion as a command post.

From this time onwards care of the garden was neglected; but eventually, in 1956, the garden was restored. It is very popular with the local Chinese and thus has the disadvantage of being crowded; you may have the feeling of being on an anthill as you make your way up and down the narrow paths and through the narrow passages.

Temple to the Town Gods

The temple, or Cheng Huang Miao, is only a short distance from Yu Yuan. Once every city and large town possessed a temple devoted to the town gods, but very few have survived throughout China. This is a rare exception. However, it is not easy to gain access to the interior of the temple, although you can usually stroll in the garden (see below).

Garden of the Purple Clouds

This garden lies at the back of the temple; its full title is "Garden of the Purple Clouds of Autumn," known in Chinese as Qiu Xia Pu, but also known as the Back Garden (Hou Yuan). The garden was originally laid out during the Ming Dynasty, later became part of a rich merchant's estate, then finally, in 1726, was made an addition to the Temple to the Town Gods. There is an ornamental lake in the park along with pavilions and some artificial hills.

The Long Hua Temple

The Long Hua Temple, known in Chinese as the Long Hua Si, is located in the southwest corner of the city in Xhongshan Nan Road, a short distance from the Shanghai Gymnasium. Here you can see the only pagoda standing in Shanghai; it has seven stories, each with a wooden balcony. The temple buildings date from the Qing Dynasty and consist of four halls with statues of the Buddha, the Celestial Guardians, and the Celestia Defenders. The surroundings are renowned for the peach blossoms in the spring.

The pagoda was first erected during the Three Kingdoms period in about 247 A.D. but was destroyed by fire in 880. It was rebuilt in 977. The present structure is of much later date. The pagoda is of brick with the exterior balconies constructed of wood. The pagoda began to develop a serious lean, but maintenance work has corrected this and the foundations have since been made firm.

The temple itself has the traditionally upswept eaves and fine supporting brackets which are a feature of southern Chinese architecture.

One of the temples has a fine example of a painted wood ceiling and a cupola.

Temple of Serenity

The Temple of Serenity, known in Chinese as the Jing An Si, is just off Nanjing Road to the north, opposite the Park of Serenity. You will know when you have arrived near the temple; there is a stone column in the middle of the road. Before the Revolution, the temple (Buddhist) was one of the richest in Shanghai, being headed by an abbot (Khi Vehdu) who had a rich wife, seven concubines, and a White Russian bodyguard. The buildings are from the late period of the Qing Dynasty but are not particularly noteworthy, and a visit to this site should be given lower priority.

Temple of the Jade Buddha

This temple, known as Yu Fo Si, has pavilions of recent date (1911, 1918), recently restored. The temple is famous for the white jade Buddha seated in the far pavilion and originally brought from Burma by a Chinese monk in 1881. There is also fine jade statue of the Buddha in a reclining position. The temple is in use again, there being more than twenty monks in attendance. Visitors are expected to remove their shoes when entering the room housing the statue of the Buddha. (Temple hours: Tue., Thurs., Fri. 8–5; Mon., Wed., Sat. noon–5; closed Sun.) There is a vegetarian restaurant next door, and a store selling religious items, both run by the monks.

YU YUAN—Key

1) Hall for Gathering Grace
2) Arbor for Viewing the River
3) Large Artificial Hill Resembling a Boat
4) Resembling a Boat
5) Tower of Ten Thousand Flowers
6) Bower of the Ancient Well
7) Treasury Tower
8) Poplar Tree
9) Garden for Learning Horticulture
10) Hall for Heralding Spring
11) Gingko Tree
12) Hall of Double Convenience
13) Double Corridor
14) Pavilion of Fishes' Pleasure
15) Arbor for Appreciating Grace
16) Bridge of Three Turns
17) Angling Terrace
18) Old Purple Rattan
19) Pavilion of Nine Lions
20) Arena for Dance and Song
21) Tower of Happiness
22) Hall for Obtaining Tranquility
23) Arbor for Listening to the Orioles
24) Hall of Graciousness
25) Tower of Elation

26) Hall of Mountain Reverence
27) Hall of Three Corn Ears
28) Entrance
29) Bridge of Three Turns
30) Office
31) Pavilion for Enlightenment by the Torrent
32) Miniature Landscape
33) Hall of Jade's Splendor
34) Tower for Appreciating the Moon
35) Nine Arc Bridge
36) Lake Pontoon
37) Pavilion for Paying Reverence to Weaving
38) Book Tower
39) Elegant Jade Carving
40) Retail Shop
41) Inner Garden
42) Temple of Tranquility
43) Fairyland of Happiness
44) Phoenix Pavilion
45) Temple of Permission
46) Tower for Observing Waves
47) Tower of Returning Cloud
48) Emerald Pavilion
49) Tower of Lasting Clearness
50) Pleasure Boat
51) Sky of Another World
52) Stage for Theatrical Performance

Yu Yuan
or Yu the Mandarin's Garden

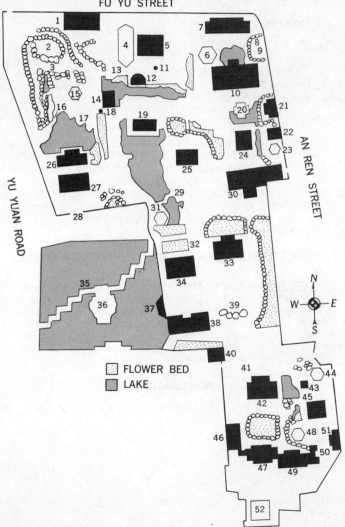

FU YU STREET

YU YUAN ROAD

AN REN STREET

☐ FLOWER BED
◼ LAKE

N
W ✦ E
S

Xijiao Park—Zoo

This park is by far the largest in Shanghai and houses the zoo, which is a well-known attraction of the city. There are hundreds of species of animal on display: tigers from the Northeast; leopards and elephants from Yunnan; crocodiles from the Yangzi; and giant pandas. Both the zoo and the park abound with pleasant gardens and stands of trees.

Fu Xing Park

The Fu Xing Park was built in 1909 and also possesses a small zoo. It is located not far from the center of the city, quite near the site where the First National Congress of the Communist Party of China was held. It is usually crowded with the residents of Shanghai and visitors from the Chinese provinces, strolling beneath the massive trees.

Other Sights

Other sights which may be of interest to the visitor are the People's Park and Square (the former race-track), the Workers Cultural Palace, the City Library, the Shanghai Radio Tower Building, and the Revolutionary Cultural Square. Your guide will be pleased to take you to these places on request. You may also wish to see Fudan University, located in Handan Road in the northern suburb. It is one of the best known in China, and can be visited upon request, along with Jiaotong University, Shanghai's other tertiary institute.

PRACTICAL INFORMATION FOR SHANGHAI

FACTS AND FIGURES. Shanghai lies at approximately the same latitude as Jacksonville, Florida. Distances: 698 miles southeast of Beijing by air, 2 hours' direct flight; 915 miles southeast of Beijing by rail, 26 hours' train journey; 745 miles northeast of Canton by air, 2 hours' direct flight; 1,130 miles northeast of Canton by rail, 35 hours by train.

Elevation: 50 feet above sea level.

TEMPERATURES

	Jan.	April	July	Oct.
Average daily maximum temperature (°F)	47	67	91	75
Average daily minimum temperature (°F)	32	49	75	56
Average number of days with rainfall	10	13	11	9
Average monthly rainfall (inches)	1.9	3.6	5.8	2.9

HOW TO GET THERE. You can travel direct to Shanghai by international flights. There are daily flights from Hong Kong (1 hour 50 minutes); there are direct services from Tokyo, Osaka, San Francisco, and New York.

If you cannot get a direct flight to Shanghai, there are many domestic flights from most large Chinese cities. Flight time is 1¾ hours from Beijing; 2 hours from Guangzhou (Canton).

Shanghai is connected to China's major rail network and has a regular passenger service to and from most important centers: 26 hours from Beijing; 36 hours from Guangzhou. It is also serviced by boat; boats leave daily from Chongqing and Wuhan. The journey takes 3 days from Wuhan, 5 days from Chongqing. There are also boat-services connecting Shanghai from Hong Kong, (56 hours), Fuzhou, Wenzhou (21 hrs.), Ningbo (12 hrs.), Dalian (36 hrs.), and Qingdao (26 hrs.).

HOW TO GET AROUND. How to Get to and from the Airport: There is no coach service available to foreigners, and you must take a taxi. Since your travel is arranged by your sponsoring agency or China International Travel Service (CITS), the cost will be included in the overall charge for a car and driver for the entire Shanghai visit.

Usually CITS arranges for a car and driver as part of your organized tour. If not, you can only travel by taxi unless you speak Chinese and know the bus routes. Taxis can be arranged by your hotel. Keep the taxi if you go shopping or to an appointment; waiting time costs very little and you will avoid the problem of telephoning for another taxi (you cannot hail them) and the usual half-hour wait for it to arrive.

There are three-wheeled pedicabs that can take two passengers; these can be fun, but again you must speak Chinese.

WHAT TO SEE. The *Bund,* now Zhonghan Road, still remains one of the great streets of the world. You will get a good view of the Bund from the top floors of the Shanghai Hotel and also from the Heping (Peace) Hotel. Stroll along the sea wall of the Bund and wander through its well-laid parks and gardens.

In the Old Chinese Town you will find the famous tea house *Wu Xing Ting,* Yu the Mandarin's Garden *(Yu Yuan),* the Yuyuan market, and *Temple of the Town Gods.*

Nanjing Road is the main shopping street. The *Art and History Museum* and the *Musuem of Natural Sciences* are located nearby and are worth a visit. Most visitors will also be taken to the *Shanghai Industrial Exhibition* and shown the vast array of products made in the area.

The People's Recreation Hall (Da Shi Jie) and one of the *Children's Palaces* are of interest; so too are the *People's Park* and *People's Square* occupying the area of the former racetrack.

Those interested in old Chinese culture may care to visit the Buddhist *Long Hua Temple,* the *Jingansi Monastery,* and the recently renovated *Yufosi Monastery,* which houses two jade statues of Buddha.

More recent historical sights include the old *French Concession Quarter, Lu Xun's Tomb and Museum,* the old American area, and the Japanese Concession in the Hong Kou district.

MUSEUMS. The **Shanghai Museum** is located at the eastern end of Nanjing Road. It possesses a valuable collection of historical and artistic objects which are displayed to show the evolution of art in China. There are four floors, covering the period from the Shang Dynasty down to the Qing. There is a fine collection of bronzes from the Shang and Zhou civilizations, a large three-legged cauldron (ding); several pieces of rare Shang pottery. There are also interesting examples of wooden tomb figurines from the Warring States period as well as a fine collection of bronze lances and swords.

There is an interesting display of Han dynasty clay tomb figurines featuring an example of a pigsty, a granary, guards armed with crossbows, some very fine carvings of ducks, horses, and dogs, as well as figures of workers with spades and soldiers with swords.

There are also some excellent pieces of sculpture from the era when Buddhism was widely adopted in China, particularly some original pieces from Dun Huang, one of the three famous centers where Buddhist cave carvings are located. There are some fine examples of the "three colors" Tang pottery, as well as Shanxi celadon ware from the Sung period; paintings and porcelains from the Yuan dynasty; paintings, porcelains, cloisonné ware, embroideries, and lacquer ware from the Ming. There is a similar range of art objects from the Qing period.

The museum features art and craft products from different provinces in China. These are items that have been created since 1949.

Lu Xun Museum: Lu Xun was the most respected and revered modern author in China. When he died in 1936 he was buried in a cemetery in the western town. In 1956 his ashes were removed and taken to the (then) Hong Kou Park, now known as the Lu Xun Memorial Park. It is located in the north of the city on Baoshan Road. There is a statue of Lu Xun seated on a pedestal in front of the tomb bearing his remains. Delightful flower beds are arranged around the pedestal.

The Lu Xun Museum was opened in 1951 in the house where the writer spent the final few years of his life, but in 1956 the museum was transferred to the present site.

In the museum you will find exhibits of his letters, manuscripts, photographs depicting his wife, family, and friends. There are original copies of correspondence with famous writers, particularly George Bernard Shaw. There are also valuable copies of Lu Xun's printed works, along with woodcuts illustrating the books; the texts of lectures, particularly relating to mass education and the reform of Chinese characters, and collections of his revolutionary writings.

Sun Yat-sen Museum: This small museum is located in the southwest of the city and was the house in which Dr. Sun Yat-sen resided when in Shanghai. He died in 1925, and the two-story building is now a museum dedicated to his life.

EXCURSIONS FROM SHANGHAI. If you want to get close to the bustling river life you can take a boat trip 25 miles down the Huangpu to the immense mouth (35 miles wide) of the Yangzi. This 3½-hour excursion on the vessel *Pujiang* is highly recommended.

Excursions further afield: Nanxiang in Jiading County (Guyi Garden; the marble boat; Temple of Confucius); to Quingpu County (Longfusi Temple and pagoda); and to Sonjiang County (Tang Dynasty stele; Xingshengjiao Temple pagoda).

There are two daily sailings along the Yangzi to Wuhan from Shiliu Pu Dock. The express boat stops 6 times and takes 52 hours; the slow boat stops 12 times and takes 67 hours. At Wuhan you take another boat to Chonqing.

SHOPPING. *Nanjing Road,* running west from the Peace Hotel on the Bund, is the best place to shop. Here you will find stores selling the complete range of goods available to the Chinese consumer. Even though you do not speak Chinese, you can go into these shops, look around, and buy the merchandise. You will find that the excellent linen, tableware, cotton sheets, and towels (designs usually poor) are good buys. Basketware, pottery products, and other arts and crafts items are worth examining. The silks produced in the region, especially from Hangzhou, Suzhou, and Shanghai itself, are superb and make wonderful gifts. There are also excellent quality silk scarves and ties, cashmere and wool sweaters, and handbags, wallets, and jewelry. Shanghai is an important printing center, and you can buy fine writing paper, notebooks, diaries, greeting cards, and calendars.

The places to begin your shopping tour are the Number One Department Store in Nanjing Road (or the Yungan Department Store) and the Shanghai Friendship Store, reserved for foreign visitors. Then try the smaller specialty shops.

The Friendship Store is located on the Bund, between the Peace Hotel and the Shanghai Mansions Hotel. It stands in an interesting area which, before 1949, was the site of the British Consulate. Now the Seamen's Club for foreign sailors awaiting the unloading and turn-around of their vessels is on the same site. To reach the Friendship Store you enter a small park through large gates and follow the path to the left. You will find the store directly ahead of you. This is the best place to begin when antique hunting, so that you can get an idea of what is available and how the prices are. Then you should go to one or both of the "commission" shops to start your search in earnest.

The shop with the most interesting collection is the *Chuan Xin Shop,* 1297 Huai Hai Rd. Central. It has a good range of porcelain, ceramics, old wooden boxes, copper ware, music boxes, pewter ware, lacquer ware, and old jewelry.

The *Shanxi Shop* in 557 Yanan Road has a large collection of Chinese and Western ceramics and porcelain ware, silverware, jewelry, furs, and clocks.

BUSINESS CENTER. Tel. 370115 at 59 Maoming Nan Road. Business executives travelling in China can make use of the Service Center for Overseas Traders which offers facilities such as translators, secretarial services, guides, telex facilities, photocopying, business introductions, consultancy services - all for a fee, of course. Located at the Jinjiang Club, the business center is jointly sponsored by the Shanghai Import and Export Trade Corporation and the Shanghai Investment and Trust Company. Open daily 8:30 A.M. to 6 P.M., except Sundays.

USEFUL ADDRESSES AND TELEPHONE NUMBERS

Frequently Used Numbers

Airport (Hongqiao). Tel. 536530
International telephone calls: Information, tel. 536266. Calls, tel. 565959.
Domestic long distance calls: Information, tel. 116. Calls, tel. 113.
U.S. Consulate, 1469 Huaihui Road. Tel. 383103, 378511.
Japanese Consulate, 1517 Huaihai Road. Tel. 372073.

Air Services

CAAC (Civil Aviation Administration of China), 789 Yanan Road, Central, Shanghai: International passenger reservations, tel. 532255. Domestic passenger reservations, tel. 533766.

Travel Arrangements

China International Travel Service, 66 Nanjing Road East. Tel. 217200.
Shanghai Railway Station, tel. 242299.
Huangpo River Tourism Service, tel. 211098.

Banks

Bank of China, Shanghai Branch, 23 Zhongshan Road. Tel. 217466
Hong Kong and Shanghai Bank, 185 Yuanmingyuan Road. Tel. 218383.
Standard Chartered Bank, 185 Yuanmingyuan Road. Tel. 214245, 218858.
Bank of East Asia, tel. 216860.
Overseas Chinese Bank Corp., tel. 213176.

 HOTELS. Shanghai's hotels offer accommodation ranging from the ultra-modern to the old and elegant, from the small and luxurious to the large and austere. The old hotels were built originally in the 1920's and 30's for use by the resident foreign communities and their guests. They recall an era in China that has long passed.

JINGAN HOTEL (tel. 563050). Located at 370 Huashan Road, away from downtown Shanghai, this hotel was recently re-opened for foreign visitors. Originally built as an apartment hotel in the 1930's for German residents of Shanghai, the Jingan features well-appointed rooms which are all centrally air-conditioned. The hotel offers excellent service and food, both Chinese and Western, and there is even an outdoor café. Pleasant gardens surround the buildings. The hotel was formerly known as the Palace. Rooms cost ¥40–100.

HEPING (PEACE) HOTEL (tel. 211244). The Peace Hotel, formerly the Cathay, is located on the Bund and overlooks the river. It is a pleasant old building with a pointed bronze-green roof. When you step inside you feel as though you are stepping back in time to the early days of the century. The reception hall is cavernous and the lighting dim. Your room has lots of wood paneling with doors leading to a baggage room, a dressing room, and a coat room. There is even a servant's room separated from the bedroom by a curtain. The hotel fittings are all made of the best old materials: brass door plates, heavy glass counters and doors, thick (but now somewhat threadbare) carpets, large chrome footrests, and old-style light fittings.

The Peace Hotel is most convenient for business executives; it is located near all the Chinese State trading corporations on the Bund. Indeed, many of them have their negotiating rooms on the eighth floor during winter months. Room rates range from ¥45-150.

SHANGHAI MANSIONS (tel. 244186). The Shanghai Mansions, located on the junction of the Suzhou and Huangpu Rivers in the heart of Shanghai, offers one of the best views of the city. In contrast, the view of the hotel itself from the Bund reveals an architectural style which, while interesting historically, is ugly. Built in 1934, it was once a smart residential hotel called Broadway Mansions. Across the road is the former Ascot House Hotel.

The hotel is seventeen stories high and stands in Wusong Road at the foot of the steel bridge which crosses the Suzhou Creek. While the service is good and the rooms spacious, the hotel has one disadvantage: it is difficult to sleep in the evenings because of the constant hooting of sirens of the river craft. Rooms are air-conditioned. Rooms cost from ¥ 35–75.

Suites are elegantly furnished in old-world style, featuring velvet drapery and Tianjin carpets. Room lighting is good; and the bathrooms are equipped with excellent showers. The view from the terrace is breathtaking.

SHANGHAI HOTEL (tel. 312312; telex 33022 BTHSGA CN; cable 0244). The city's newest hotel, located at 505 Wulumuqi Bei Road, makes an interesting comparison with its namesake, the Shanghai Mansions. The 30-story building provides accommodation in 600 air conditioned rooms, each possessing a telephone, color television, and modern amenities. The main dining area is on the 23rd floor: separate restaurants provide Chinese food (at Wang Hai Lou or Restaurant Overlooking the Sea), as well as Japanese, and French/European cuisine. A separate banquet room seats 450 diners.

The hotel is convenient to both Nanjing and Huaihai Roads; there is a bus connection (No. 48) to the Bund (about a 12 minute ride). Room rates are ¥ 50–60 (double), ¥ 125 (suites).

JINJIANG HOTEL (tel. 534242). This fine old-style hotel, similar to the Peace Hotel, is located in the old French Quarter; it was formerly a hotel for French residents of Shanghai. Three new buildings have been added, making it the largest of Shanghai's hotels, with 800 rooms. The grounds within the walled complex are superbly maintained. The oldest building, the north block, constructed in 1931, features grand wood-panelled rooms, Old-World elevators with white-gloved attendants, and palatial dining rooms serving superb Chinese and excellent Western food (try the yogurt). The hotel has two coffee shops, hairdressing salons, and the usual array of service facilities, including a telex room. The hotel is also well known as a landmark in modern history. In the modern building flanking the courtyard, Zhou Enlai and President Nixon negotiated the 1972 Shanghai Communiqué, opening the way for the restoration of full relations between China and the United States. Located at 59 Maoming Road. Room rates vary from ¥ 35 (single), ¥ 65 (double), to ¥ 150–300 (suites).

INTERNATIONAL HOTEL (tel. 563040). The International (formerly the Park) is an imposing 24-story hotel overlooking the Renmin (People's) Park and located at 170 Nanjing Road. It is about a mile from the Bund. The hotel used to be well known for its fashionable daily tea dance and its famous chefs, and—in more recent times—because Mao Zedong used to stay there on his visits to Shanghai. Now it is best known for its excellent restaurant. Rooms cost ¥ 35–80 per day.

CYPRESS HOTEL (tel. 329388) The Cypress or Longpai Fandian is another recently constructed hotel. Located near Hongqiao Airport at 2409 Hongqiao Lu, and about 30 minutes from the Bund by car, it has been built on the site of the former Shanghai Golf Club. The Chinese restaurant (Bamboo Room) features Sichuan food; the Silk Road restaurant serves Western-style food. There are 161 rooms with rates ranging from ¥ 80 (double) to ¥ 160 (suite).

OVERSEAS CHINESE HOTEL (tel. 226226). Also located in Nanjing Road north of the Renmin (People's) Park, this hotel, as its name suggests, is usually reserved for visiting overseas Chinese. It is located just to the east of the Park Hotel.

CLUBS. The International Club at 65 Yanan Road West (tel. 536954) possesses small but well-kept grounds featuring rock gardens, ponds, stone benches, and even garden swings for adults. There is a small restaurant with less than ten tables serving food of a reasonable standard. Private rooms may be booked for banquets.

Sporting facilities are good. There is a 25-meter *swimming pool,* open in the summer months only (15 June–20 September); two outdoor tennis courts; an outdoor basketball court; and a billiard room. Have your hotel check the hours that you may use these facilities.

The Jin Jiang Club, tel. 370115 (55 Maoming Nan Road), is also available for use by visitors. The club possesses an indoor Olympic pool, tennis courts, billiards room, games room, and other facilities. Formerly the Colonial French Club, the building features superb art-deco interiors. There is a restaurant and Business Center (see separate listing).

RESTAURANTS. Shanghai has hundreds of restaurants preparing dishes in all the varying styles of cuisine found in China. The best banquet restaurants are those located in the hotels, particularly those at the Peace, Jinjiang, the Jing'an and the International. They are all first class and are frequently used by Chinese officials to entertain foreign delegations. One rank below, but of fine standard, are the banquet restaurants at the Shanghai Mansions, the International Club, and the Shanghai Hotel (Wang Hai Lou). The best restaurants located outside hotels are given below. The first three serve the finest Shanghai dishes available outside of hotel banquet rooms. The others are the best ones serving regional specialties.

OLD TOWN RESTAURANT. 242 Fuyou Road, tel. 282782. This famous old restaurant, known in Chinese as Lao Fandian, possibly serves the most authentic Shanghai cuisine in the city. Located in the old city, near Yu the Mandarin's Garden, the restaurant provides an ideal place for lunch after visiting the Temple of the Town Gods, the Wuxingting, and the Yuyuan itself. The restaurant dining room can be reserved (well in advance) for a banquet where up to twenty-five guests can dine; prices are not low. In exceptional circumstances, it is possible to have the restaurant hold an evening banquet in the Yu Garden, providing guests with an unforgetable experience.

OLD PROSPERITY RESTAURANT. 566 Jinjiang Road, tel. 293153. This small but long-established restaurant, called Laozhengxing in Chinese, is also famous for its Shanghai cuisine. Try the crab, freshwater fish, and turtle.

YANGZHOU RESTAURANT. 308 Nanjing Dong Rd., tel. 225826. Superb Shanghai cooking, particularly seafood. Book early; there is only one private dining room and it is one of the most popular restaurants in Shanghai. Try the wild duck.

XIN YA RESTAURANT. 719 Nanjing Rd., tel. 223636. A famous old restaurant providing good regional dishes, but specializing in Canton cuisine. The ground floor is a cake and pastry shop, the restaurant being located on the second and third floors. Some of the old waiters worked there before the Revolution and speak good English. Service is excellent.

RED HOUSE WESTERN FOOD RESTAURANT. 37 Shaanxi Road (South), tel. 565748. Here the influence is distinctly French. Standard favorites such as cocktail de crevettes, tournedos, and even crepes suzettes and Grand Marnier soufflé. The maître d'hôtel is fluent in English and French. Formerly known as "Chez Louis," called the "Hongfangzi" in Chinese. Prices are high. Located only a few minutes walk from the Jinjiang Hotel.

OTHER RESTAURANTS. There are many other restaurants in Shanghai that you may care to try. Some of them are listed below.

Luyancun. 763 Nanjing Road East. Tel. 537221. Jiangsu cuisine; also Sichuan dishes.

Meixin. 314 Shaanxi Road South. Tel. 373919. Cantonese; the fried rice is superb.

Gondelin. 43 Huanghe Road. Tel. 531313. Vegetarian; an attractive old restaurant.

Moslem. 710 Fuzhou Road. Tel. 224273. Moslem-style dishes.

Hunan. 28 Xizang Nan Road. Tel. 285454. Hunan dishes; spicy.

Sichuan. 457 Nanjing Road. Tel. 221965. Spicy Sichuan-style cooking.

Chengdu. 795 Huaihai Road. Tel. 376412. Features spicy dishes.

SNACKS. Shanghainese delight in snacking at the hundreds of small restaurants specializing in these sweet and savory delicacies. Join them and try the steamed dumplings filled with minced pork; fried beef dumplings; steamed rice dough stuffed with delicacies; eight-jewelled rice; and sesame cakes. There is one place where the snacks are delicious and the young clientele interesting: Taihu Fandian, 432 Sichuan Road, near the Peace Hotel.

 COFFEE, CAKES, AND SUNDAES. Some visitors to China get a craving for good coffee, cream cakes, and ice cream sundaes. If you are one of these your prayers have been answered. Go to the eighth-floor dining room at the Peace Hotel. There you will find the best coffee in China and, amazingly, perhaps the best creampuffs and chocolate éclairs you are likely to taste anywhere. The ice cream sundaes are good, too.

If you would like to try the cakes and pastry that the locals eat—the people of Shanghai are well known in China for their 'sweet tooth'—then you should go to one of the following shops: the *Donghai,* 145 Nanjing Road East, near the south wing of the Peace Hotel—it is a rendezvous of the well-to-do youth of Shanghai; the *Deda,* 805 Nanjing Road (West); the *Kaige* in Nanjing Road—formerly Niesslings. These are all well-known, but if you can't find them, go into any of the multitude of cake and pastry shops.

BANQUET SUGGESTIONS

You can eat superbly at the Peace Hotel, either à la carte or at a banquet. Should you wish to get together with your friends or repay the hospitality of your Chinese hosts, you can arrange a dinner or luncheon by ordering the banquet menu suggested below. Alternatively, leave the choice entirely to the chef. All you need do is advise the hotel desk of the day, time, number of persons attending, and the cost per head (does not include drinks), usually 24 hours in advance. A less elaborate menu than the one given below may be ordered about half a day in advance.

The following menu would cost you ¥ 50 per guest and would be suitable for eight or more people.

Chinese	Pinyin	English
冷盘	Lěng Pán	Cold Hors d'Oeuvres
三丝烩干贝	Sānsī Hùi Gānbèi	Scallops with Three Kinds of Shreds
串烤虾片	Chuànkǎo Xiāpiàn	Prawns en Chemise (Jackets)
茅台鸡	Maótaí Jī	Maotai Chicken
冰糖银耳	Bīngtáng Yíněr	Fungus in Crystalized Sugar
金丝烧卖	Jīnē Shāomài	Steamed Dumplings with Golden Shreds
双色草鱼	Shuāngsè Cǎo Yú	Fish with Two Colors
素扒四样	Sùpā Sìyàng	Four Kinds of Vegetables
柴把鸭汤	Cháibǎ Yā Tāng	Duck Soup

NOTE: "Maotai Chicken" is chicken cooked using the potent Chinese liquor, but you need not worry about the effects—all the alcohol has evaporated by the time the dish reaches its final stage of preparation.

This menu, and variations on it, can also be prepared by the chefs of the Jing Jiang, International, and Shanghai Mansions hotels.

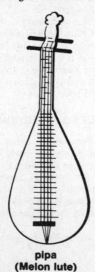

pipa
(Melon lute)